TIGHTROPE
TO THE MOON

ADVANCE PRAISE FOR THE BOOK

'Startups are a household word now but very little is understood about the journey that the founders take in starting a business from scratch and then living their conviction day after day. *Tightrope to the Moon* takes readers through the reality of starting up and the pressures that must be overcome to survive and succeed'—Naveen Tewari, founder, InMobi and Glance

'The founder's mind can be their best friend or worst enemy. Sitting on top of the world starts from carrying the world on your shoulders. This book is a rare commentary on how a founder's mind works, and what keeps it strong and steady in the storm of uncertainties'—Vijay Shekhar Sharma, founder, Paytm

'Thousands of startups get funded in a country like India. A select few go on to become category leaders. What separates these few winners from all the other founders who set out with similar ideas and resources? When stripped away completely, this question lays bare the one element that makes all the difference—the nature of the founder. This book takes us one step closer to understanding why some founders are more successful than others'—Ramakant Sharma, co-founder, Livspace

TIGHTROPE TO THE MOON

HOW **MEGA FOUNDERS**
WIN THE **STARTUP** WAR

RAHUL CHANDRA

PENGUIN
BUSINESS

An imprint of Penguin Random House

PENGUIN BUSINESS

Penguin Business is an imprint of the Penguin Random House group of companies
whose addresses can be found at global.penguinrandomhouse.com

Published by Penguin Random House India Pvt. Ltd
4th Floor, Capital Tower 1, MG Road,
Gurugram 122 002, Haryana, India

Penguin
Random House
India

First published in Penguin Business by Penguin Random House India 2024

ISBN 9780670097012

Typeset in Adobe Garamond Pro by MAP Systems, Bengaluru, India
Printed at Thomson Press India Ltd, New Delhi

www.penguin.co.in

MIX
Paper | Supporting
responsible forestry
FSC® C010615

To my mother, Sumati Chandra, who taught me to focus on the positive qualities in people and ignore the negatives. She would have made a terrible VC, but she was the most compassionate mother I could have asked for

To my father, Ishwar Chandra, who has touched so many lives with his kindness. You taught me to step fearlessly out into the wide world and make it home. I now know how hard a job it is to be half as good a father as you

Contents

1

Startups Are Shaping Our World

'The best ideas come from solving your own problems.'

—Alexis Ohanian, co-founder, Reddit

I have been evaluating founders for twenty-five years. One way or another, I have been involved in decisions that led to investing nearly a billion dollars in startups. These decisions have led to companies whose value is more than $10 billion. In this period, I would have heard pitches from 3000 founders and worked with sixty-five startup teams as a board member.

I have been on calls with founders during my meals, in the morning, before I sleep and even during my wife's labour pains. When I started as a venture capitalist, it was a small world that founders lived in. They were a minority and so were venture investors like me.

Now, startups are everywhere. They are evident in the cabs we ride in, the content we watch and the food we order.

They are the fastest creators of wealth and value in the modern world. Since 2008, the nature of tech entrepreneurship has changed from creating technology to make technology businesses smarter to making human lives smarter. The power that enables car owners to earn from their depreciating assets (Uber), home owners to cover their mortgages (Airbnb) and content creators to monetize their creativity (Instagram and Netflix) is based on models that connect many consumers to many providers over platforms built for the new era of humans interacting far more comfortably with technology.

The scale at which humans have adopted technology is hard to imagine. Startups that built these new services have outsized their traditional business competitors. The new world is expected to be dominated by technology startups that will disrupt how humans consume.

Startups that cross $1 billion in valuation are termed 'unicorns'. At the peak of startup valuations in 2021, the combined value of unicorns was nearly 10 per cent of the aggregate Standard & Poor's 500 (S&P 500) market capitalization. Much of this value was created in a period of less than five years. Private investors with billions of dollars at their disposal estimated this value on the basis of the potential that these startups would achieve. The scale of equity value created per year was unprecedented in economic history. Whether this value correctly reflected the intrinsic value of the asset is not as material as the huge amount of optimism and expectation that accompanies startup growth.

The scope of what technology can create is always expanding. Startups in emerging markets and frontier markets in Africa and Asia are working on creating an impact in the lives of hundreds of millions of consumers. Investment dollars are more than willing to move from pockets of low return to riskier equity in high-performing startups. Capital to convert ideas to reality is available for everyone. Startup valuations in the private markets are inefficient and future promise-dependent. A single large investor or a clutch of many small investors can decide what a loss-making company should be worth. They rely on their estimation of future value and assign a valuation that would not stand scrutiny on a basic conventional finance valuation modelling sheet. Yet the flow of capital ensures that the valuation is validated by the next incoming investor and then the next. The flow creates cascading valuation jumps, and in a few years, a startup with the right trajectory of growth could be a mega outcome worth billions of dollars. Successful startups have created an army of wealthy entrepreneurs. Startup employees are also pulling in millions of dollars from employee stock options.

The best part of this wealth creation process is that it does not discriminate. Anyone from any background can take a crack at solving a problem that will improve lives, lower costs or increase speed. Religion, location, education, colour and sex are not a factor. Founders are creatures who identify a problem that is sometimes personally experienced but is exclusively understood at a depth that only founders can reach.

Founders, especially those with a technical background, engage with a problem in a way that is unique to them and in the process, develop a deep connection with it. The dogged pursuit of an answer to the question, 'How can this be done better?' leads to fantastic results. Their motivation to pick and stick with a problem for years is rarely based on the urge to make a quick payday. It is driven by their ownership of the problem—a belief that they have been chosen from amongst millions of people to find the solution. The biggest problems when solved yield billions of dollars in company valuation. Thousands of startups try but a successful startup is rare. A unicorn is even rarer. Of all funded startups, a unicorn could be as rare as one in 10,000. But if this status is achieved, a founder can move from living a lower middle-class life in an obscure town to living the life of a billionaire in the most expensive part of a metro, all well within their thirties. Private plane commutes, fancy cars, custom-designed real estate and legend-level reputation are part of the success story. The founders who make it big are the titans of the startup world. Many others struggle to pay EMIs and live within 'just enough' means. The first set are written about. The second set are rarely talked about in public.

There is no insurance for entrepreneurs. Failures cost real time, money and lives. Not failing but not succeeding either costs even more. Cost is measured in immense emotional units.

Those who deliver scale of impressive magnitude and can sustain it end up creating enough wealth to make their investors rich. They become the reason why new investment capital keeps flowing into this high alpha return, power-law business. They are the 0.001 per cent in their class. They have a vision, they convince investors, employees and customers to follow them over hills and rivers and finally deliver everyone to the promised land. They are vulnerable and lifetime learners from failure. They take a long-term view of business growth but move as if the world were ending tomorrow.

From the seed of an idea in a founder's mind, a startup slowly takes shape, and as it grows, it employs thousands, becomes a household brand and has millions of customers. Isn't that fascinating? It's happening all around us. In our lifetime, we can witness the creation of potentially many multigenerational businesses. All from a thought, a never-give-up attitude and with a little help from investors.

Energy transforms into matter when slowed down enough. In a startup, what is this energy? Where does it come from? How is it sustained?

It's not the capital. There are examples of bootstrapped companies like Zoho, Atlassian and GitHub that went on to create mega outcomes without using traditional venture funding. It's not the idea. Many ideas have been written on restaurant napkins but only a few see the light of day and even fewer become real companies. It's not even the ecosystem—some of the most successful startups like Canva, Rovio and Spotify originated in places that are devoid of any Silicon Valley vibe. The common factor across all startups that convert an idea into a billion-dollar company is the founder's resolve and ability to achieve success against countless odds. Founders go through long periods of uncertainty and, more often than not, wake up to a day that is the opposite of the previous day in its rhythm and stress. It is impossible to predict a founder's day as each one sees new situations and challenges. Founders steel themselves against this stress and become more immune to uncertainty as they go through the formation years to the growth years. This superhuman behaviour is at odds with how most humans are wired. The human brain craves predictability as numerous functional MRI-backed studies have concluded. Humans thrive in predictable situations and can build tremendous stress in uncertainty. In contrast, founders become adept at dealing with uncertainty. As stress comes flying thick and fast, founders train their mind to keep their cortisol levels moderate, stay in the zone and focus on solving problems.

A founder's mind is a deep, dark well. In its crevices rest the secrets that when parsed reveal the ideal behaviour pattern that could create mega outcomes. Just like professional athletes, founders are a combination of traits, which compound with time—some were formed when they were children and some from the time they started their venture. Some traits are inherited and some come through nurturing. This complex response system residing in a founder evolves with every input and situation. Founders are dependent on this response system. Their responses are shaped by their natural conditioning and their self-awareness to reorient themselves for different outcomes. Some traits are so deeply tied to the founder's personality that they can either become the core reasons for success or the Achilles heel that can cause a perfectly sound startup to lose steam and wither away. Some other traits can be modified and honed to deliver outcomes that matter. These are identified through deep self-awareness and a desire not to repeat past mistakes. It takes tremendous willpower to prevail over the initial pain caused by pattern change. The startup a founder creates is dependent on how they process, how they plan, how they let go, how they motivate themselves, how real they remain despite training their mind to defy reality and how they react to ethical questions.

Founders are also on a journey of self-discovery to identify how their behaviour leads to varying outcomes on three axes— pain and stress created in and around them in the process of building, time taken to achieve lasting success, and number of lives left before game end.

There are many stories on how brutal the early part of this journey can be. The initial excitement wears out and the reality of the emotional and economic demands that a startup imposes on the founders and their families starts to test the steeliness of their resolve, day in and day out. Pain and stress take a toll in the form of deteriorating health and mental well-being. It is rare to see a founder without a bulging belly and dark circles under their eyes. Irritable bowel syndrome and chronic acidity are common complaints after years of unhealthy eating habits. Nervous system stimulants are more commonly used than before, adding to the already prevalent alcohol abuse problem that many founders deal with. I recently sat across from a founding team pitching to me in a meeting room. One of the founders maintained a zoned-out smile for the entire duration of the hour-long meeting in which he did not say a single word but also didn't lose eye contact for even one second. I have seen people high on substances, and I can tell the difference between a bright-eyed fully attentive participant and an 'I do not want to lose my shit so I will lock my expressions and hyperfocus on the conversation' participant. Another founder would have multiple nights of non-success-based highs in a week and by 2 a.m., the size of the company he wanted to build would grow from $1 billion to $10 billion. By 3 a.m., he would be telling his team that they were building a $1 trillion business.

By late morning, they would remember that they did not even have the early signs of a product-market fit.

Long periods of uncertainty and working countless hours create immense stress on the founder's family. Unmarried founders get unfettered hours in the office, often crawling into their sleeping bags on the office floor at the end of a long day. Marriage adds a new responsibility of reciprocal companionship but not the need. Founders whose marriages survive are fortunate to have spouses who understand the grinding reality of AWOL partners. Many successful founders have a hard time switching between the hero worship they receive in the office and the complaints they receive from their spouse for never being present and shirking household tasks. Marriages become hard to sustain, and there are periods of extreme stress when the home is a battleground while a façade of normality is maintained in the office.

The time taken to achieve lasting success varies for different businesses, and founders often realize after the first few years that the journey is actually much longer than they thought it would be.

A unicorn founder whose family lived in another city told me that during the startup's early years, he thought he would maintain this long-distance arrangement for a year or two because after that he would find a buyer for his startup and then would go join his family. Those one or two years became seven or eight years. At some point, he must have realized that he had to decide if he would rather wrap up in two years and head back to his family or stick around for an unforeseen period of time.

Founders also have to make choices that could bring their startups close to death. Maintaining a high cash burn or turning ultra conservative by cutting back on growth is a critical decision. In the death-defying manoeuvre of pulling a startup out of a nose dive, a founder could pull up a tad late and end up hitting the ground and exploding into a blazing ball of fire. Venture capitalists (VCs) push for growth, having banked on the emotional undertaking of the founder—that of building a business at breakneck speed, no matter the cost. Burn high, grow fast and raise another round before the plane hits the ground is an unspoken rule of engagement. Driving a loss-making startup through exhilarating growth and pulling a fresh funding round just before flaming out is a rare skill that some founders master while others need bailing out and a game reset with a new life.

Founders live many lives and are reborn every day as a more mature and evolved version of their previous selves. Their audacious existence is worth a close examination for the scale of ambition and resilience that it summons and sustains. The human mind is a mystery. It makes us respond in ways that are inexplicable. It helps us overcome hopeless situations and gives us strength we never knew we had. There are two pertinent questions to ask: Why does the mind do what it does and what does it do in certain situations?

The dive to understand the mind of a founder can be futile. In this book, we will not attempt to decipher the why. We will leave that to the extensive scientific research that is being conducted with ever more fearlessness at universities and labs around the world. We will lay out the what: What is the founder's response in situations that give them an edge and helps them create mega outcomes?

2

The Key

'I am the master of my fate, I am the captain of my soul.'

—William Ernest Henley in 'Invictus'

Founders choose their goal and the outcome of their journeys. They can take paths leading to larger outcomes by choosing new flywheels or markets and products. Or they can trade off a bigger outcome for lesser risk and take the path that offers more certain outcomes.

In the pursuit of larger outcomes, founders take paths that elongate the journey. Paths get riskier as they get longer but the payoff of ending up with a larger and more successful outcome can be thousands of times more rewarding than small and successful ones.

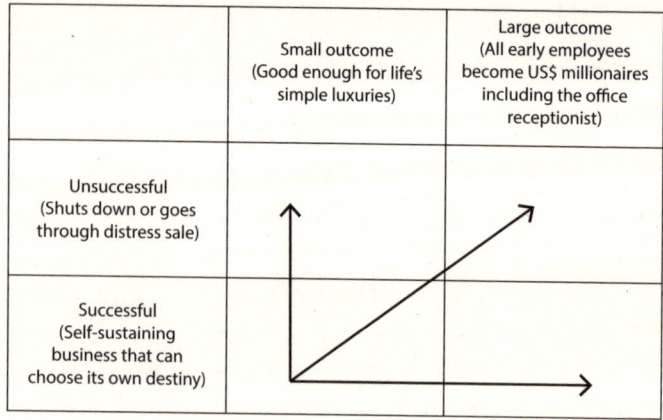

	Small outcome (Good enough for life's simple luxuries)	Large outcome (All early employees become US$ millionaires including the office receptionist)
Unsuccessful (Shuts down or goes through distress sale)		
Successful (Self-sustaining business that can choose its own destiny)		

The founder will determine if the final outcome is 10,000x or 1000x or 1x. Founder evaluation is the persistent factor for people like me who are investing amidst the uncertain criss-cross of technology cycles and economic cycles.

Startups can grow without money from VCs and be successful, but as they do not prefer external dependence that can help accelerate execution, they follow a slower path to building value. This pace to success is steady and slow because the founders choose to first build a profitable business and then reinvest capital for growth from the free cash that the business generates.

More commonly, with so much venture capital now looking for opportunities to back promising businesses, a founder can choose to grow faster than what self-sustenance allows for. Investor capital provides the opportunity to prove that the startup has a product-market fit and take the product to more and more customers while burning cash at alarming levels. The cash-burning journey can derail the already fickle fortunes of a zero to one startup. No matter how good the founder is, a startup's ECG frequently comes close to flatlining. Minor and major blips appear frequently and can cause a chain reaction that puts the startup in a death spiral. External capital is the jet fuel to grow as well the life jacket to survive. To corral capital, the founder seeks meetings to pitch their plans to VCs. Until 2021, the term 'venture capitalists' was used to refer to a small, full-time, dedicated group of people taking high risks to make exceptional returns on their investments in new companies. Now it refers to a wider base of risk-friendly investors who want to participate in the pool of investments going into startups. In the five years between 2018 and 2023, $2.2 trillion was invested globally in startups. When VCs are fortunate enough to get past the pressure from the fear of missing out, they spend days and weeks evaluating their investment decisions. The venture-investing decision is a combination of feedback from the rational mind as well as on instinct. The rational decision takes in market analysis that smart brains spit out after chewing on any data that can be put into Excel pivot tables. Instinct feeds itself on the research consumed by the rational mind and then seeks feedback on aspects that cannot be understood by the rational mind— the most important being the founder's ability to deliver a successful return on the invested capital. Founder quality measured by instinct is the decisive nudge for VCs to select one startup from amongst many others, all of whom could get funded if only the rational mind was on the job. Founder quality is an amorphous factor but is industry-specific and peer-benchmarked. It is hard to assess objectively. It can be confused with stage presence. Glib talk and polished answers can create an impression of mental clarity. Impression can be reverse-engineered by smart founders. Founders aping Steve Jobs in black turtlenecks and using quotes from his biography as their own are relatively easy to spot. Harder to spot are the founders using the question bank method—they map feedback from friends on which VC likes to hear what and then make the right noises to nail the pitch. The pretenders can create an endearing image to appeal to the topical expectation of investors—a pretence of frugality in down markets or thump the table in world-conquering bravado during go-go markets.

In VC investing, it is rare to see the perfect trinity: a situation where the investor can say, 'I love the market opportunity (I rate it A+), I love the business model (I rate it A+ also), AND I love the founders (and even this is A+).' This trio ensures that the biggest possible outcome is achieved with no one factor acting as a constraining factor. Whenever the trinity happened in my lengthy investing career, it almost always resulted in a big-big outcome.

If two of the three play fickle, the only one worth getting right is the founder quality. If the right founder is backed, they will manage to find the A+ market with the A+ business model.

Let's say two founders jump into chasing the same opportunity in the same market using the same business model. The difference in the founders' vision can steal away the big funders from the competition, virtually drying up all resources for the competition and giving a free run of the road ahead. By discovering new flywheels of growth that multiply the size of the eventual shape and form of the company, the outcomes can be vastly different for the same type of business in the same market. In the same space, between two startups fighting for turf, one founder will build a company that will become only large enough for another founder to acquire them.

Hard and confusing as it is to assess, founder quality is the single most important criteria for making successful investments. Founders can crash and burn a company with infinite access to capital (WeWork) by carrying their once useful delusion mindset into areas that need them to snap out from distorted reality to authentic reality (like the business' ability to deliver profit margins).

Founders can not only navigate near-death startups away from danger but can also find value creation in unexpected areas.

PocketFM was launched in 2018 to provide quality audio content across genres. The initial capital was spent in acquiring lots of listeners who could use the app for free. Monetization was tough in the first two years and by the end of 2019, despite users spending more and more time listening to content on the app, only three months of cash was left in the bank and new funding looked tough. The founders got a new funding round closed with only a week of cash left. Most people had not only written off PocketFM as a company but also the audio content space as a category. The PocketFM founders found a way to massively scale content by translating Chinese and Korean audio series. In 2022, they took PocketFM to the US market. This move was risky but it paid off in spades. In 2024, the company was tracking a revenue of $150 million a year.

In situations where the market is not large enough or customer adoption is slower than expected, founders can catch a new tailwind that is bigger than the original bet and change direction to reach a bigger outcome. Founders have guided startups caught in market shifts (One97 expanded from providing value-added services to starting Paytm for doing payments), customer shifts (Zomato moved from restaurant review to food delivery) and model shifts (Lenskart moved from online sales to omnichannel sales).

Founders walk into a VC's office with the reference of common friends carrying the only asset they possess—the potential energy gained by their decision to go after an opportunity. Most of them are taking entrepreneurial journeys for the first time. In the social status-conscious startup world, most of them are as yet 'non-entities'—unknown names in the sea of others on the quest for success. They are desperate to prove that they have higher potential than the next team that walks in. The VC arena is a world of judgement. Founders are evaluated on the basis of their past successes, depth of thinking, clarity of thought, vision expansiveness and execution abilities. The founders introduce themselves to the investors—pedigree, attractiveness of their vision and the intimate relationship they share with the problem statement. Meanwhile, the investors switch between the rational and their instinct: seeking patterns that match those of past successes, remembering mistakes made in rejecting teams that went on to mega outcomes, mapping skills to roles, assessing the founder's trustworthiness and X factor.

Founder evaluation is not the sole agenda in the pitch meeting but it has the biggest impact on the investment decision. In a pitch, founders throw a lot of information to establish their credibility. They can list industry leaders as advisers. Advisers have no skin in the game plus they have their own day jobs, hence they don't matter. Founders love to talk about their angel investors and brag about who they were backed by. Some angel investors are so prolific that they appear on every other startup's shareholding or cap table. The relevancy matters if the founders have worked for or with their angels and have built enough trust to go back to them to ask for an investment. Other angels who matter are domain specialists—experts in their field who were intrigued enough to look under the cover and were impressed enough to invest. Founding teams talk about their collective backgrounds. They share their work history and how they got together to start.

The investor can consider the collective strength of the team. This view can take away attention from a sharper evaluation of the founders. All put together, there are far too many signals for the VCs to process efficiently. So evaluation comes down to ignoring the irrelevant signals.

All co-founders are super important but they are not equal. The group is led and held together by a single individual. If the group formation is unclear on this dynamic, it would end up compromising the forward movement that the startup needs.

In the investing world, there is comfort in backing startups that have multiple founders. This is because a team of founders tends to do better during stressful times as they can draw from each other's strengths. Co-founders complement each other, take on the building of vital pieces of the business without depending on hires, and despite the overlap of responsibility, they are not interchangeable. The co-founder configuration is a delicate balance of weight-carrying that is established based on past patterns of interaction between the group. The behaviour, competence and ownership levels of the founders are drawn to the fore in time-tested situations. Co-founders break up into two groups—the first group features the 'Key', who acts as the keeper of the spark, and the second group comprises those committed to building a fire from the spark.

The Key is the nuclear reactor responsible for providing infusions of energy in the startup as it makes its way along the erratic path to growth. A Key pulls the startup forward and sets the pace. Other co-founders may be able to emotionally afford to move at organic speeds, but the Key will take on the role of the impatient horse in front of the wagon. When others have written off the future of the startup, the Key will be the last one standing in a burning forest.

The Key will use Steve Jobs' famous reality distortion field and inspire the team to perform at their peak especially when the going is rough. They are the most likely to set the tone for the culture of the organization. They set the bar high. They are often the emotionally most edgy about hiring leadership outside the founding team. They also tend to be emotionally volatile, engaging in hair-pulling drama at the smallest misstep. Most likely to end up divorced by opening bell on listing day, the Key breathes vital life force into an idea even if it means sucking it out of their own life. A Key juggles the acuteness of execution, the vision of greatness and the daily uncertainty of building a company with ease. A Key leads through example by bearing the biggest brunt of frugality required in the cash-scarce periods.

If the Key is removed, the configuration fails, just as if the planet that has the maximum mass and the strongest gravitational field is no longer around to keep the solar system in balance.

Co-founders around the Key are critical for success, but startup failure can be attributed only to the Key's ability (or lack thereof) to lead and execute. The co-founders play important roles that help the startup execute faster, but the script is written by the Key. Co-founders tend to rely on the Key for energy sustenance. They have blind faith in the Key. They know that their Key is not perfect, are aware of competency and personality gaps, and step in to fill them. The co-founder configuration is also designed to allow freedom of movement of vision and execution. The Key goes back and forth defining and redefining the vision, stepping back to manage the day-to-day functioning of the organization and wandering off to raise capital. Co-founders make sure that the startup is executing to plan, day after day after day. The Key relies on the co-founders' execution focus when they represent the startup to investors. The Key represents the entire co-founding team to the investor they are pitching to. In rare cases, two co-founders are conjoined so tightly that separating the Key becomes difficult. They choose to be one tightly knit unit for the external world. They take equal risk and pump in equal energy to fire up the startup.

In the twenty-five years that I have been evaluating startups, I have met thousands of founders, from all backgrounds, ages and approaches. Professionals with thirty-year careers behind them. Just-graduated teams. Single-founder teams. Raised an obscene amount of seed financing but still no idea, no direction teams. Running both B2B and B2C models in one-company teams. Will only hire family teams.

Stealth forever teams. Second-time teams but only out of sheer boredom. Will sell at the first instance teams. Founder living in the US because their children are still in school there but the market is in India teams. Can raise capital but cannot execute teams. Can execute but cannot raise capital teams. The A team in B markets. Frugal teams, listening teams, arrogant teams, been-at-it-forever teams. The list is long. But when I look back at the journeys and outcomes of investments made, the mistake I made the most often was to decipher team strength by processing a barrage of signals about all founders and advisers and angels but not by focusing at a microscopic level on the Key. This bit me hard when the startups where I felt comfortable with collective founder strength were in fact hiding the lack of a strong Key. What was supposed to be a Formula 1 vehicle turned out to be a car in a carousel. A weak Key means no one is pulling the load forward. Everyone is working hard and there is plenty of activity, but no one is losing patience. No one is throwing up their hands in frustration. No one is screaming at 2 a.m. about delays that should have been avoided.

In some cases, the mistake I made was to assume that the shortcomings of the Key could be supplemented by hires. Building a strong team around a founder so they can be left to do their visioning is not an alternative to a strong Key. Hires can't fix this problem. Maybe some co-founders can, but even that is wishful thinking. Maybe in these instances the valuation was too good to pass on and caused my rationalization to override my doubts about the Key.

The Key should be the focal point for determining the potential of the startup. Spreading attention to the whole, believing the whole is greater than the sum of the parts can be an expensive diversion for the already strained analysis mechanism of the investor's brain. If the Key can be identified and assessed accurately, then we have taken the first step towards understanding the biggest non-Excelable part of the investment puzzle, and, if I may say so, the greatest predictor of a billion-dollar outcome will begin to come within our grasp.

The exercise can be tricky, but is easy when practised and remembered. Look for the one who lives in the past, the present and the future. The Key is most often the person who thought of the idea. They were there on day minus zero. They die the most for the startup but also move the furthest from their natural state in doing so. They are the ones who go through the pains of labour to give birth and are also the ones who will lead the startup through its one to 100 stage by making sure that they evolve and grow fast enough to sustain the startup's growth. This personal growth is a journey of letting go of the ego, transforming hardwired natural behaviour patterns and hardest of all, opening themselves up to the scrutiny and judgement of those who they lead.

Imagine that this crazy person is offered a big reward for running across a desert devoid of any shade or water. They can un a distance of their choosing, but the rewards are proportionate to the distance run. They are under no compulsion to either run at all or to run a minimum distance. Their desire to run is based on the motivation to win a big reward. They could run a mile or a hundred miles.

Now for the rules. If there is a medical emergency in the middle of the desert, irrespective of distance chosen, no medics will come to provide aid. A slow, miserable death writhing on the hot sand, begging for water is almost guaranteed. No maps are provided, no compass. A vague promise of a water station is given on the condition that sufficient progress is made, but the organizer could redefine 'sufficient progress' on a whim. The crazy runner has to convince the water station manager that the chance of not collapsing while running miles under the desert sun is non-existent. And now for the most fun rule. If the runner chooses to risk death by running as fast as they can, covering a long distance at great speed, then the water station manager would be favourably disposed to doubling the water quota. If the water quota doubles, the runner can run even further and take the even greater risk of running fast. They can keep repeating this and win really big or face exhaustion and death.

What is more, the runner has to carry in their backpack several items dear to them—their family, their health, their ego, any nest eggs they may have built, their social life, glorious weekends, self-respect and sanity. Oh, there is another requirement—the runner must ensure that a group of followers that is tagging along must also make it to the finish line. They must share their water and rewards with these followers.

The odds are beyond crazy yet many brave runners attempt this wild race. Many perish. The craziest ones choose to run ultra-long distances and attain mega status. They chart their path through the desert. They make it to the finish line in good time, do an exemplary job of convincing water station managers that they will finish strong and get plenty of water. They keep everyone following them in good spirits. What they did with their baggage is hidden from most but in order to win, they had to lessen the load. What makes them choose the crazy distance in the first place? Are they trying to prove something other than physical prowess? What massive irrationality sets them off across the vast desert for a reward that can be so elusive? What energy reserves do they tap into to charge themselves and their contingent, who choose to keep running alongside them in the debilitating heat? What mindset pushes them to keep taking that one step after another, a million times over? How do they ignore their blisters? How do they keep the vision of them crossing the finish line at the front and centre? And most importantly, what were their personalities like at the beginning of the run and what are they like at the end?

Once we have identified the Key, we can identify some of the traits that set them apart. Over the last twenty years,

I have consistently observed certain specific thinking and response patterns in Keys. These traits are demonstrated in dire situations, in winning big, in causing trajectory inflection and in giving wings to people. By no means recommended for deriving causation, these characteristics are present in such an uncanny pattern that it makes me wonder if there is a link between them and the Key's success in creating market leaders worth billions of dollars in equity value.

3

The Need to Prove Ourselves

'Memories are never entirely silent.
They murmur in your cells, shadow the mind,
knock at the door.'

—Nicole T. Smith, *We Have Shadows Too*

We all share a common code. We were all born programmed to feel the same need. The need to prove ourselves. Most of us break a few bones in the process, and a few of us don't stir from our comfortable perches after considering the trouble involved in scratching that need. Achievement of any kind needs hard work. Achievement is habitual. Achievement is compounding. First in class, winning sports championships, completing building projects, cracking highly competitive entrance examinations, self-taught virtuosos—people prove themselves in many ways.

Creating a startup is probably the peak of productive action stemming from ego-driven behaviour. The efforts of a Key are aimed at producing the biggest outcomes. What code variation leads to such off-the-chart approaches to a common need affecting most of humanity? Are Keys designed differently? Do they react differently to the same stimuli? Are Keys destined to be Keys irrespective of their origin? Or did something happen in their origin that helped transform them into a Key?

Keys to whom I posed the question, 'Why bother creating a startup and going through a painful journey?' gave a similar response: 'I am creating something massive, and I cannot afford to fail until I have proven it.'

Keys are unhinged people. They are cut from a different cloth. Their code *is* warped. Their need to prove themselves far exceeds that of most of us. They may appear self-assured but their stress levels push them to operate on three hours of sleep. They never complain about their unpredictable fortunes. They don two personas—an inner person who carries self-doubt and suffers gut-ripping stress, and an outer person who remains positive and excited about building their dream. Keys who lie on the far end of the need to prove themselves have a shot at becoming Mega Founders.

Mega founders build massive businesses, solve a problem for millions of customers and create value in billions of dollars.

Keys have amazing mastery over stress and retain control of the constantly exploding situations in their startups. This level of wiring is so unique and innate that it's hard to ignore the role of childhood experiences in shaping the founder's personality. While many deny any specific childhood experience that pushed them to chase the infinite, their never-give-up attitude and stress-taking ability can be traced back to how their personalities were forged when they were young. As children, they became champions at achieving wins against stressors by taking control of situations through self-regulation and their problem-solving skills.

Founders

If human existence were naturally blissful and childhoods were full of joy, wonder and love, then the need to prove ourselves would be non-existent. But the world is not built for the universal satisfaction of everyone's needs. The need to prove ourselves against other humans is itself a grand obstacle in realizing our innate joy. If all was well in the world, we would be a happier race, but the path of progress would not be controlled by our will. We would be satisfying our hunger by eating ripened fruits picked from the ground every day and for every meal. The mismatch in our needs and wants and the unequal distribution of goods is at the heart of our existence.

The quest for universal love, while hidden deep inside us, is an elusive state. Even if all humans agreed to not eat each other's meals, a lifestyle of siestas and blissful fruit-picking would be quickly disrupted by other animals who would compete for the same fruits. This would trigger the amygdala—the part of our brain that detects danger to tell us to gather more fruits than we need and drive away the annoying herbivores. In such a world that recognizes resource scarcity, few of us would build our clans with members who cannot fight to fulfil their needs. Some of our clan members would still experience their anterior insular cortexes lighting up in empathy with the hunter who, after losing his leg to a Smilodon's bite, spent most of his time in his cave. Perhaps motivated by the need for greater good, some of these clan members would build carts to transport the fruits back to the settlement. The brains we live in and the society that has emerged over thousands of years has enough stimuli to have us act towards solving for scarcity and inclusiveness. Between fear's first responder—the amygdala—and the altruistic anterior insular cortex, we are all pre-programmed to labour for change.

So we all want to change things around us because that is how our brain responds to the environment but where does the need to prove ourselves come from? The need to find a connection with something bigger than us.

All of us carry different levels of anxiousness to prove ourselves. A conditioning reason could be at the heart of this anxiousness. Erich Fromm connects this anxiousness to 'separation' embedded in human nature. Humans were dependent on nature for thousands of years. Only in the last few hundred years, we have created societies for ourselves that skip this deep-rooted link. In his book *The Art of Loving**, he connects the deep-seated memory of lost oneness that humans feel with nature as the cause for a perpetual state of anxiety. This anxiety nudges us to leave a permanent impression in the world around us.

When human society co-existed with the animal kingdom, we instinctively adapted to find oneness with nature. In *The Art of Loving*, Erich Fromm writes that 'Man has transcended nature—although he never leaves it. His pre-human harmony is irretrievably lost and he must find a new harmony'. We are programmed to overcome our separateness and aloneness. 'We are aware of our helplessness before the forces of nature and society. The experience of separateness arouses anxiety, it is, indeed, the source of all anxiety. All this makes our disunited existence an unbearable prison.' Is the desire to develop a startup driven by an inherent need to reduce our anxiety by finding oneness with a greater purpose?

---

* Harper & Row, New York, 1956, p. 7.

Ann Masten, a prominent developmental psychologist, has conducted extensive research on the response to stressors by children and adolescents. She is the author of the book *Ordinary Magic: Resilience in Development,*[*] a professor at the University of Minnesota, and the director of the university's Project Competence research lab. She has conducted longitudinal studies on children who have experienced a range of stressors. Her research indicates that children's sense of mastery and control has the most positive effect on their resilience. Also, the presence of even one supportive adult relationship can help children build strong identities around their abilities. Her list of these factors includes capable caregiving, close relationships, problem solving + planning, self-regulation, emotional regulation, motivation to succeed, faith/hope/ optimism, belief that life has meaning, and routines and rituals. Executive function in children is the sense of competence and belief in their ability to influence their environment. Children who have a sense of mastery and control are better able to regulate their emotions, set goals and solve problems effectively. Ann Masten's research has shown that even in highly stressful environments, those children who have executive function are likely to develop a resilient core when they feel nurtured by various psychosocial protective factors. As adults, our ability to deal with stressors is the continued sense of mastery and control over situations that we develop as children.

_____

[*] Guildford Press, 2015, 1st edition, New York.

As we embark on life's journey, the road forks a bit more often than when we are nearing the end. The choices we make are driven by us taking leaps based on an estimation of our capabilities, which may be off or on the mark. The need to prove ourselves varies in intensity and depends on personal capability and freedom to choose our paths. As humans we often err when it comes to making an honest assessment of our capabilities. We tend to either underestimate or overestimate our ability to achieve. The path to prove ourselves can end up being disappointing in both cases. In the first instance we are bored by achieving too easily and in the second, we are left frustrated by not even coming close to our aspirations. Choosing an easy path despite high ability will lead to boredom and lingering remorse over a wasted opportunity. Choosing a difficult path but not having the ability to follow it causes disappointment. Those of us who most accurately map their capabilities with the path they choose to prove themselves achieve the most enduring match. Founders choose the most difficult path to prove themselves *and* are able to match this choice with their ability.

Childhood stories are buried deep in our memory. Our elders tend to remind us only about the happy parts. The unpleasantness of our stressors are not remembered accurately or pushed back in our memory. These stressors bring varying degrees of mastery and control to us as children. Many childhood experiences shape our personalities. Different levels of sadness and trauma are in store for all of us in our cosmic lucky draw. By an accident of generational hand-me-downs, inherent nature, incidents and role models, each of us chooses a different mechanism to fight back and win. Childhood experiences impact each of us differently, depending on our support network, attitude and ability to regulate emotions. Those children who can master the situation, with ability or doggedness with some help from a loving supporter, will build a resilient core. As these children grow older, their strong resilient core enables a journey of self-growth. They can deal with the high degree of stress that comes with their choice of path and continue to be effective. They are not geniuses who have all the answers. Their childhood was like everyone else's but they choose to draw out the most difficult curve on life's path.

What situations did they encounter in their childhood that intensified their need to prove themselves to a level most humans would not bother with? What stressors and psychosocial protective factors did they encounter that led them to develop the degree of resilience needed to achieve their goals as adults?

Twelve-year-old Smalltown Studious had just finished his final exams. Always one to live up to his name, Studious put in more hours of studying than any other child in his class, in his family or in the neighbourhood. During his final exams, he had deprived himself for days of any entertainment. No TV. No gaming. No play. Just cramming and solving one maths problem after another. Now, with his exams done, he rushed home filled with excitement, impatient to turn on the television and enjoy hours of watching Doraemon. He couldn't wait to eat the treat that waited for him at home—to celebrate the end of the exams, his mother had cooked his favourite, poha. He came home, carelessly chucked his bag in the corner of the cramped room, and settled himself on the bed in front of the TV. His mother gave him a warm hug and brought out the hot poha. He leaned back against the pillow as he ate, guffawing loudly at Doraemon's antics. Unexpectedly, his father came home early. Doing odd jobs to make ends meet since his shop had to be closed down, his mood swings had taken a southward turn. He was irritable most of the time, and the malaise that accompanied him everywhere accused him of a failed life. His eyes fell on the discarded bag on the floor and then on the pre-teen sprawled on the bed enjoying his poha—having too much fun in life. The next moment cast a shadow so deep on the boy that for the rest of his life, he would not be able to look at poha with the joy he had felt earlier that day. Fun became an awkward, guilty activity from then on. This situation was a stressor but not entirely unusual. Many fathers can't bear to see their kids having unadulterated fun. This boy was not average, though. His emotional response was to achieve self-sufficiency with focus. An unwavering focus whose foundation rested on stubbornness. Inspired by the resoluteness of Eklavya, the boy learnt to do what he could do best—work hard to score high. He was beset by the need to control outcomes, the need to grow out of his tiny home and, most of all, by the insatiable need to be appreciated. This trauma, replayed year after year, became a tsunami of powerful emotions that the boy learnt to manage and channel.

Suburban Superkid lived in a sprawling urban mess with his parents and two younger siblings. His parents had worked for as long as he could remember. His father was an assistant engineer in the electricity board, and his mother taught physics at the university. Their home was so far from their offices that both parents had to leave by 6 a.m. to reach work on time.

As the eldest child, whenever his parents got caught up at work, the responsibility of looking after his siblings landed on Superkid. Which was every other day. This meant waking up earlier than anyone else at home, finishing up his school work, packing paranthas and sabzi in his siblings' tiffins and getting them ready for school. The school bus would not wait, and time had to be managed precisely to accommodate his somnolent sister's lethargic movements and his brother's tendency to throw up his breakfast if he ate too fast. Juggling the numerous balls of time pressure, cranky dependents and parental expectations wired Superkid's brain to perform tirelessly at expanded bandwidth. The pressure immunity was so strong when it came to managing dependency that Superkid never thought of it as a chore. It was natural to handle the stress of managing people to move towards a common goal—catching the bus on time.

Natkhat National grew up in nine cities, changed seven schools and anchored his comfort to change. His friends spoke seven different languages, followed five religions and had home situations starkly different from each other: matriarchal, patriarchal, orphaned, joint, nuclear, inter-caste, inter-religion. He had seen enough to not even notice diversity. He could walk into unfamiliar situations and feel at ease instantly. With a mild-mannered father exploited by a system that emphasized only the transferable in his transferable job, Natkhat was exposed to Bharat darshan at close range. Every time the family unpacked, settled into their new home and grew new roots, it would be time to pack up again and depart. The family's belongings would find their way back into the black metal trunks stencilled with a long abandoned permanent address. Natkhat's comfort with landing in a new location, making it home and restarting had built a core of positivity that had been strengthened by many tearful farewells and images of temporary homes disappearing through the tiny back window of the rickshaw that coughed its way to train stations. Natkhat knew no fear, and the stress of new situations did not faze him. He would always be the new boy in class with the most friends and the richest stories to share about his experiences.

Delhi Daredevil's neighbourhood uncle had bought a new car. It stood parked on the side of the entry lane of the middle-income family Delhi Development Authority colony. The Mother Dairy milk-dispensing booth was just past this lane. Bleary-eyed in his hand-me-down sweater, holding a can for milk, Daredevil stood mesmerized by the sleek red and black Japanese car. His family still barnacled on their infinitely powerful Bajaj scooter. One after another, a family member would add their weight upon its tiny wheels and it would still move like an obedient donkey. They were a circus stunt, but it felt normal. Until this damn Maruti turned up in their middle-class existence. Maruti uncle was no epitome of sensitivity. Secretly, he enjoyed making people squirm. Young boys unsure of their place in the world were the easiest to rattle. Maruti uncle crowned his satisfying morning regimen with a walk in the municipal garden. After making enough throat-clearing noises to wake up the neighbours, he would set out to fetch milk from the dairy. Seeing Delhi Daredevil standing there staring at the car was enough to trigger him. 'Do you want a car like this one?' As Daredevil nodded excitedly, the winning jab went straight to the heart—'Look at it as much as you want but your father won't be able to afford one of these even if he worked all his life.' As the barb sunk in, Daredevil's inner voice boldly echoed in the dark corridors of his brain—'Uncle, one day I will not only own a Maruti but also the showroom that sells it. Not only the showroom that sells it but the factory that makes it. Not only the factory that makes it but the company that owns it.' An inadequacy took root. Inadequacy not of money but the smallness others make you feel when you don't have enough.

Does everyone in Studious's, Superkid's, Natkhat's and Daredevil's shoes grow up to become a Key? Do some of us focus our energies better to achieve the crazy dreams that will help us prove ourselves to Maruti Uncle? Did the sight of poha strewn on the floor create a razor-sharp focus to achieve greatness? Why is this not true for everyone? What unique strain lights a fire in the darkest moments of unfair denial and deprivation? I don't know the answers. Then why do I write these stories? Because they are the childhood tales of some of the mega founders whom I know. Did these incidents or circumstances shape them? Perhaps. When I asked them to describe their childhoods, they emphasized these incidents as turning points in their lives. They carry these strengths and scars throughout their lives. Their chosen paths are tough, and they developed the resilience to withstand the stressors early in life. If those blessed with a sharp mind combine their self-inflicted pressure of focus with the power of infinite hunger to prove themselves, then why won't it convert energy into matter? Those of us who do not carry the massive need to prove ourselves but have high capability and focus end up thriving but are not constantly pushing the envelope on creating mega outcomes. We make great career climbers. Those of us who carry the massive need to prove ourselves and can combine capability and focus can become Keys driving mega outcomes.

What do high-degree-of-difficulty paths look like? When a youth who spent a childhood with limited means starts to earn a decent income, it would be normal to expect that the fulfilment of material needs should provide a sense of security. A home, a nice car and a secure future should naturally be considered worthwhile goals to aspire for. This is true for most of us, but not for founders.

Founders ditch all these for an uncertain future because they left the security of a home multiple times to make a new home every time their belongings were packed into black trunks. Holding on to the protective blanket of the familiar is not a need. They are happy to leave one to find the next because they are convinced that there is more than one blanket, and they will find one sooner or later. Moving to an unknown, making it familiar and then moving on to the next one is a norm. Parents marvelling at Elon Musk's mega achievements and hoping their kids also launch rockets should not freak out when their children display Elon's double or quits mindset. Elon risked most of his earnings from his successful sale of PayPal when he redeployed them into a nascent company called Tesla.

Founders are comfortable juggling multiple balls and managing their EMIs, families and employees. Each ball suspended in the air is just like the glass of milk they held with one eye on the clock as they urged their younger siblings to pack their school bags. Founders often pack their days with design, product specifications, finances, hiring and regulatory applications, and it is a wonder how someone with no prior experience can get their arms around a completely new set of problems. Making unlimited bandwidth available for a long list of activities is a superpower. Watching their ability to manage across the board gives their employees and co-workers comfort. They see a leader whom they can rely on. After all, motivating people who are dependent on them has been a practice since childhood. They are comfortable with the idea of people depending on them without it being a chore. With conditioning to use an empathetic response to this dependency, it becomes a lifelong attitude of responsibility.

Founders risk the predictability of a pay cheque because they feel they are being underutilized and exploited by the providers of the pay cheque. Their calling is not in this safe zone but in ventures that will yield super-sized outcomes. The pay cheque is not enough for them to go back to their three-bedroom apartments and feel a sense of achievement. They would rather build financial value that outsizes their world by an order of magnitude. They want to poke Maruti Uncle in the eye with their net-worth certificate.

They jump in headlong to take on challenge after challenge because if they succeed, then the undeniable proof of their worth will be conveyed to those who did not recognize it. To prove that their life amounts to more than what they have been given credit for, they have to be driven by the refusal to accept failure. By adopting a never-say-die attitude, they believe the poha strewn across the floor can be magically returned to the bowl that their moms handed to them with unconditional love in their eyes.

In spite of the conditioning of their childhood stress triggers, Keys are not immune to stress. Like all of us, they also face their demons every day. Like the uncommon phenomenon of post-stress growth, they use their stress to build strength. They are good in an area that gives them mastery and control. They are not disheartened by childhood traumas but emboldened because they had the support of some unsung loved ones who believed in their ability to change their situation. They set goals. Crazy goals. They develop an unwavering sense of confidence to achieve these goals. They are resilient in the face of disappointment. They build themselves into beings who keep levelling up from the Maruti to the showroom to the factory to the company that made those cars.

Heroism comes coupled with tragedy. Keys take roads that help them prove themselves: initially to the people who are supposed to love them unconditionally and later to the phantom who sits on their shoulders, judging them on a measurement scale that even they don't know why they chose for themselves. The dogged pursuit of the undefined takes its toll. Those who build extraordinary outcomes also suffer the consequences of dissatisfaction and constant hunger.

Personalities committed to achievement seldom rest in complete bliss. Devoid of any other emotion, they live with the handicap of infallibility. The compulsion to always 'think big' causes extended periods of rudderless exploration because most regular-scale feasible options are suboptimal life goals.

Many broken parts of the past lie just beneath the quiet surface, disturbed only by their rapacious breathing. In another life, the soul could be lightened by putting these pieces to rest but then the world would be denied the mega outcomes that these founders end up creating.

4

The Goal

'Mount Everest, you beat me the first time, but I'll beat
you the next time because you've grown all you are going
to grow . . . but I'm still growing.'

—Sir Edmund Hillary

I remember a founding team telling me that they could easily
make a million dollars (net of tax) every year from the services
business that they had been running. Aside from driving
around in BMWs in their twenties, these Gurgaon-based
founders didn't feel a sense of achievement from running this
business. When I met them again a few months later, they had
junked what they had built and started afresh in the developer
products space.

Not all entrepreneurs have a mega need to prove
themselves. They are happy to build lifestyle businesses and
not chase growth. They are done as soon as their aspirational
lifestyle is achieved. Then they maintain their empire until

their progeny takes over. And if their children show no interest in taking over the 'family business', then selling it to a partner or winding it up becomes necessary.

Founders set hard-to-achieve goals and then back that up by never giving up on achieving them. Their goals are tough, even impossible.

Why can't founders just set simple goals? Goals like 'before the age of thirty, I will own a fancy car', or 'before I turn thirty-five, I will buy a nice apartment in a fancy neighbourhood'. These goals are perfectly capable of fulfilling childhood fantasies and leave room for a more balanced life. It is hard to fail at these goals except by choosing a lifestyle where keeping a decently paying job is a challenge. Of course, these achievements would amount to short-term joys that would wear off more quickly with every subsequent success. And there is a long pecking order that culminates in an S-Class Mercedes and a five-bedroom apartment in Gurgaon's fancy golf course neighbourhood—'DLF V'. Making one's way up the order could easily see one to the other side of fifty.

Our founders want to jump a few ladders to get straight to the top of the board. Their goal of building a large outcome needs long-term chasing and is crucial in delaying the vacuum that comes with 'now what?'. After achieving the humungous targets they set for themselves, they keep repeating this exercise until there is no more room to grow. Then they start another business and repeat it all over again. The scale of ambition is not dependent on any external factor. Neither capital nor market size nor team. Because ambition is a matter of choice. It exists without factoring in what cannot be done. Only what can be done. Whether it results in a commensurate outcome or not is immaterial. If external factors are unfavourable, ambition will drive the founder to change course, level up or restart—no matter which way the wind blows, ambition will keep pushing the founder forward.

What does a scale goal mean for a founder? No available measure helps project the growth rate for a business that has no comparable. There is no industry or competition so that rules out a rate to beat. In the absence of past patterns, founders leap into the darkness with their proclamation of 'bigger, better, faster, cheaper'.

Several years ago, we had invested in an e-commerce company. The business was blowing through cash as if it were going out of style. It had pushed on growing orders month on month when every order meant adding to the burn. The investors had heartburn from the spending but had agreed after much back and forth to give the company an emergency lifeline.

I had spent an exhausting hour and a half talking to the founder of this e-commerce company whose fragile startup had just come back from a near-death experience. The discussion was whether to have a growth plan that was moderated so as to have enough cash left over to survive, or whether to let the market drive the growth based on the demand potential. The former was driven by a long-term view of building a business that was throttled by reducing the burn-generating offers and discounts available to customers. The latter was a way to find the market potential that would then determine the growth rate. It would certainly cause a repeat of the cash-out situation. The founder argued that in the absence of any history (these were the early days of e-commerce), a defined growth plan would fail to prove the market potential. The following day, he went back to growing as much as the market would take. The argument was flawed if judged on the premise of building a sustainable business. But it was right when it came to setting a goal. The sales growth that this business demonstrated was an eye-opener. It gave a brand new view on the size that this business could grow to. The discovery was expensive, of course. It burned a lot of cash at a time when capital was not easy to raise. This is not a recommended way to set a goal. It is the most bizarre demonstration of how founders think of setting goals. In this case, the mindset was 'how high can it go?'.

When we sit down to write an exam where we can choose the questions, do we set the hardest exam for ourselves? When founders set out to prove themselves, they set the bar so high that they will almost certainly fail. This paradox of wanting to prove oneself but choosing the hardest goal possible is unique to mega founders. When there is so much at stake, why set yourself up for failure? These hardest of goals take many forms as the business progresses from an idea to a rapidly scaling-up business. In the early days, the goal is a business achievement that will ensure that the 'first step' out of the gate is a spectacular success. When the founder thinks of the problem they are trying to solve, there is a natural urge to outdo any existing solution by an order of magnitude. Ten times more, a hundred times faster. Toppr, an ed-tech platform that provided learning courses and entrance exam tutoring, increased the number of questions in its question bank tenfold to 40,000 to give the largest choice to students preparing for the IIT Joint Entrance Examination (JEE). Old-world test prep companies were pushing their limits with a question bank of 4000. The goal at this stage was also set in the context of customer delight. This was why Zomato's original version put together a customer delight experience by aggregating reviews of 1400 restaurants for the Delhi-NCR region. This made it the most exhaustive resource for customers. The FreshDesk founder was deeply familiar with the complexity that customers had to grapple with when using CRM products available in the market. He went the other way to build the product that was easiest to implement and use. Simplicity was the goal.

Like all of us, the founder's goal orientation exists on two planes—what in common language would be called rational and irrational thinking-led. For most people who have spent a few years in the business world, something that is 'rational' is considered positive and long term while something 'irrational'

is looked upon as negative and short term. The value-laden
terms 'rational' and 'irrational' do not exist in psychology
books because research indicates that most of our actions are
not guided by such deliberation—we depend on emotions,
heuristics and automation. Decision-making occurs separately
from the cognitive-led system.

A founder's mind alternates between rational and irrational
as they move from short-term to long-term goals. In the short
term, it leans more on the rational to identify and deliver
the proof points in the product validation stage. The founder
breaks down a customer need to a specific set of features. The
product flow is carefully chosen. The effort is estimated and
divided amongst the founding team. A rational approach is
followed to complete a basic version of the product within the
resources available. The mistakes are granulated and cleaned
up. There is no glossing over. Whiteboarding is not the
end—product conceptualization and design end with a
working product.

The founder makes rational choices by deciding who the
customer is and the scope of the product. In the rational frame,
the customer fits a specific definition. He is found in a specific
place. The customer in a *kirana* store. The customer is in a rural
household owning three or four cows. The customer is a commuter
going to a factory in Tumkur. The customer is a young working
adult with a small amount of surplus cash but no engaging way

to start saving it. The framing of the customer in specific terms narrows down the zone of the goal-setting. The founder selects from a large basket of choices and then hyperfocuses on his choice.

The scope of the product is also defined rationally. What exactly is the product expected to solve? From a long list of possibilities, the founder decides which single feature will create the biggest impact for the customer. The product helps create a digital point of sale for the kirana store. Or the product helps you find the most nutritious cow feed at the best price. Or it helps you book a ride at the lowest cost per kilometre. Or it lets you invest your savings in digital gold in less than forty-five seconds. The process of elimination is guided by the founder's judgement, which is based on their knowledge of the customer's needs and the potential of the product to deliver hard, measurable outcomes like speed and ease of adoption. There is a leap of faith in choosing, but it is accompanied by a quick and limited check that the specific product solves the specific need.

The product could have been anything but is now defined tightly around one utility. Like customer framing, this tight definition for the product also narrows down the zone of the goal-setting. The team can now get hyperfocused on fine-tuning the product vis-à-vis the customer requirement.

The founder now looks for response to this choice of market and product. The cold start. Yes, the product solves the problem, but how do you get the customer you chose to *buy* it? By now, the founder also has proof of their ability to convert a need to a specification and deliver proof of a product based on the strength of their engineering skills. The validation comes as a small but critical achievement.

Validation is received in the form of customer adoption rates that retain momentum on new users and depth of use.

The rational part has proven the core. It has produced the base ingredients with which a chain reaction has to be created. A chain reaction to set the irrational goal.

The initial success with the basic product provides feedback that is enough to spur the founder to set the long-term goal. Founders let themselves drift in the irrational plane until they find a goal that matches their grandiose ambition. Their need to prove themselves pushes them to find the widest footprint of customers, products and markets.

Filters are dropped to come up with the most broadly encompassing customer definition to maximize market size. The founder is now in unleashed mode. Founders use their ability to see patterns in seemingly unrelated concepts and ideas to make this leap from the rational to the irrational. Associative thinking, a mental process where the mind connects ideas, concepts or memories based on similarities or connections between them, is enhanced by brainstorming.

The brain is able to match customer needs, customer types and product capabilities in a dynamically iterative matching process. A part of the brain is ingesting, chewing and spitting out patterns at incredible speeds.

The market definition of the product changes from an online taxi company catering to intercity travellers to encompass anything that can be moved—food, groceries, goods for pick-up and deliveries—and on all types of vehicles. It expands to needs like this across multiple countries. In OYO's case, the market went from discount hotels in Gurgaon to building their own hotels to owning hotels in Las Vegas to creating a new brand in a hyper-competitive market like China. Any budget traveller around the world became the customer. Rational thought cannot cause such a shift in defining the opportunity.

Just one year into its formation, Zomato changed its name from 'FoodieBay' to build on a vision that was much bigger than the original. Its founder explained that his decision stemmed from 'hitting a wall and needing to jump over it'. Zomato covered restaurants in five cities in India at that time, but he spoke of entering countries outside India. The company decided to take a short-term hit on killing the brand because it could not transcend food. The capital they had raised at the time of making this grand proclamation was only $1 million. With only an early sign of success and no big funding to ride on, the founder talked about pursuing an ambition that sought global markets and a much wider opportunity set.

One97 was a mobile value-added service business with a net profit of Rs 50 crore in financial year 2012. No consumer had heard of One97. Only in the labyrinthine corridors of telecom companies did some commercial team members know of a Nehru Place-based vendor called One97. In 2010, One97's founder Vijay Shekhar Sharma launched a consumer-facing service of a mobile wallet called Paytm. It took him only four years to set a high bar on the consumer brand when he told the media that his ambition was to create a brand that would last beyond his lifetime and was loved by people across the world.

Ola's founder stood differentiated by his ambition. He competed with five Indian online cab companies that were launched simultaneously and with Uber, a global startup with far cheaper capital access. He fought a tough fight to win the Indian cab market against a heavily funded global competitor. Uber relinquished the China market and doubled down on India. Growing into new cities, launching three different grades of cars and adding more cars than competitors, launching two- and three-wheelers finally led to a steady state in which both Uber and Ola hold an equal share of daily taxi rides in India. The Ola founder could have rested on this achievement. With a $100 billion outcome in mind from the start, he looked at driving revenue from every use case that a network of moving vehicles could extend to, including ownership financing, entertainment and demand fulfilment. This goal for Ola Mobility was before Ola Electric came into being.

Lenskart was the zeroed-down outcome for its founder after he simultaneously built multiple promising unrelated revenue-generating businesses that could have become large outcomes. One business took online orders for powered glasses from US customers, custom-made them in India and shipped them to dealers in the US for distribution. The other was an online classified site for college students that solved any issue a student might have. Lenskart.com, an online eyewear retail site, was set up in November 2011 along with Watchkart and Bagskart. The founder shut down everything so he could put all he had into the spectacles business. Lenskart, now one single business, sells eyewear worth an estimated Rs 2000 crore a year.

The most magnificent part of how a mega founder sets a goal is how he makes the world believe in its rationality. For the hypothesis to become a reality, calling out the goal is the first step in mustering the resources to realize it. Throughout history, conquerors like Alexander and Napoleon have taken on impossible tasks and found an army ready to back them.

To do this for successive new waves of wannabelievers, to determine the logical foundation for this irrationality that can stand the scrutiny of countless sensitivity analysis Excel models and armies of MBA graduates and to delay the realization of the big reward when the small reward is right there—that is the magic that mega founders deliver with their goal management. The need to defend this impossibly huge long-term goal is a great exercise to retrospectively add more logic and reason. The goal could have been influenced by the emotionally-driven desire to build a $10 billion company or a $100 billion company but that is illogical by itself. Then building upon the original thesis of a mobile ad network, online taxi service, a budget hotel network, a mobile wallet, restaurant listing, the product was expanded to become the largest lock screen on smartphones/largest mobility network in the world, a global provider of hotels for small businesses with the largest inventory of hotel rooms. As more doors opened or tailwinds appeared, the push in the original direction opened the wedge to bigger markets.

Audacious goals inspire people because by following them, they can be part of a once-in-a-lifetime story that they can tell their grandchildren. Try hiring a senior leader by telling them that you are building a very sound and solid business with an expected value outcome of $100 million. You will draw a set of risk-averse people. Now change that to a $100 billion company. Fortune-seekers will appear from nowhere. It is the same for investors. When the risk is equal in both cases—both choices having a one-in-a-million chance—you might as well bet on the bigger outcome. And if an investor is convinced about a $100 billion value outcome, then they can justify spending a few billion dollars to take a ride on this train. With the ability to hire the best and the power to raise billions, an impossible goal is more likely to lead to larger value creation than a solid but definitely small goal.

Mega founders who set these audacious goals are missing a fear gene. In the building up of an outsized return, they can become prisoners of their own personas. Faced with an option to close out the marathon with a smaller than planned but more certain outcome versus the same impossibly huge goal with no certainty in sight, founders can ignore the needs of those who followed them—an employee who does not have job certainty in a ten-year-old 'startup', or an investor who can still lose money in a business that has a valuation of billions of dollars but lacks an undercarriage for a safe landing. Should the founder relegate their original goal in favour of real and tangible, albeit smaller, success, or should they continue to throw the dice to deliver the promised outcome, and, in the process, risk everything? Many boardroom battles have been fought around this debate between safely rational and dangerously irrational.

Irrational thinking is self-corrected by the natural human need to be logically consistent. Just like anyone else, a founder would be sceptical of another founder's crazy goal. Emotionally, they too respond with incredulity to a goal that sounds illogical. This emotional response sets a standard of reason on irrational thinking. Founders want to sound rational even if their goals are preposterous. When tennis pro Novak Djokovic sets himself a goal to do a calendar grand slam, he talks about how it is a huge challenge, his willingness to embrace it and to do everything in his power to make it happen. Mega founders use this method to think explicitly about their goals by publicly speaking about them. By the time the goal is repeated for the 617th time to employees, investors and the press, it starts to make more sense to everyone.

The mindset that founders use to navigate the duality of rational versus irrational is 'good delusion'. When the 'good delusion' is pushed to areas that need less delusion and more reality, this mindset becomes harmful for the founder and the startup. Goals are rarely scaled back even though outcomes can be a fraction of the original plan. There are course corrections that can positively impact focus. With cash resources to fund these distractions, the original goals tend to get inflated by side projects so ridiculous that they could have been only dreamt up either while sitting on the pot or after some late-night, ego-inflating discussions. Lenskart dropped all other product categories, focused on eyewear and went omnichannel. Ola finally dropped the UK and Australia markets. Oyo got out of China.

The inability to switch from good delusion to reality is a founder handicap caused by the pain avoidance that comes from remaining constantly detached from reality. Founders lose the ability to think in the grey zone, seeing situations as all good or all bad. They may ignore evidence that challenges their belief. Founders tend to forget that the fight to overcome their need to prove themselves was won a long time ago but they just did not realize it in the blurry battlefield of goal-setting.

5

May Saraswati Reside on Your Tongue: The Power of Articulation

'Don't be afraid. Yes, you can do it,' he said.
'Get your mind around it. You can do it.'

—A very calm Steve Jobs to a stunned
Wendell Week, CEO of Corning,
when placing the first order for the
not-yet-commercially-produced Gorilla glass

The spoken word is one of the most powerful forces available to mankind. Words chosen well can weave thoughts into a virtual tapestry of mythical objects, making real the imagined. Speech guides the brain to take a journey into the unknown and participate in the speaker's quest.

Startups are thoughts to begin with and nothing more. They are given shape through words. And the founder's imagination is shared through these words with the people who will help make it real.

Eloquence has been studied from the times of the Roman orator Cicero, who wrote in *On Invention* about how the 'good orator is truthful, knowledgeable, and persuasive'. In 350 BC, Aristotle wrote a book in three parts that expounded on the role of rhetoric. Scottish philosopher David Hume was convinced that complex ideas can only be explained by eloquence.

Mega founders are verbally dexterous by nature, preparation or experience. They are constantly thinking of the world ahead and do not have the luxury of lazy comparisons. They have to define new concepts, unfamiliar ways of execution, unprecedented valuation asks, new business lines and experimental go-to markets. Their words are their tools when they have nothing else. Being good with words is not to be confused with having good language skills. It is the outcome that matters. If you can get the audience to believe in your ability to deliver a large outcome then no one cares whether you make grammatical errors or freely mix two languages. However, irrespective of language, the one element that stands at the heart of every persuasive communication is rhetoric. According to Aristotle, a persuasive speaker must be seen as knowledgeable, trustworthy and morally upright. In trying to persuade and win over investors, employees and customers, a founder most commonly uses deliberative speech— akin to a man in a square in ancient Greece advising the audience to do something or warning them against doing something. The audience has to judge things that are going to happen in the future, and they have to decide whether these future events are good or bad, whether they will cause advantage or harm.

Aristotle describes three types of rhetorical appeals that form the basis of the art of persuasion: ethos, which appeals to the credibility of the speaker; pathos, which appeals to the emotional state of the audience; and logos, which appeals to the logic of the speaker's argument.

When a founder goes to raise funds for their startup, VCs like me are usually connected to them via a common friend—another investor or a founder whom we have backed in the past. The belief in and comfort we have with the introducer rubs off on the unopened package. This provides a starting base of ethos for the founder. Personal stories of 'been there done that', comparable work experience, or perhaps a direct experience of customer pain helps build the ethos up from the base. The founder weaves pathos into his pitch by freely expressing his emotions and his heart- and soul-fuelled quest for the glory of victory. In using logos, the founder backs their belief with evidence in the form of company achievements or recent data that supports their claims. Many conversations by founders rely only on logos to try and persuade a star contributor to join or an investor to write a cheque.

An idea is seeded because the founder's brain has joined the dots across unrelated areas that most of us fail to observe as obvious connections. Tired of observing things being done in the same way year after year, batch after batch and predictably leading to the same issues, the founder's brain visualizes possible solutions. Why continue repeating the exercise in the same painful way? How can I rearchitect, repurpose and reformulate this age-old pattern? The question leads the brain to see the pieces of the jigsaw but they don't fit. After many sleepless nights, the bulb will go off and finally, the jigsaw will rearrange itself, fitting neatly into the correct grooves. So now the solution is visible to the brain's eye, but this is just the beginning. The jigsaw is only the approach to solving a problem and not the solution itself. This approach as well as the problem and its magnitude need to be explained to another human being. 'In words'. The founder will attempt to do this in the beginning with people who are familiar with the problem. They could belong to a network that introduced the founder to the problem or explained it in more detail.

They come to the conversation with the benefit of context and a pre-existing motivation to believe in the credibility of the founder. This set is likely to get the approach to solving the problem with less difficulty than those who have no context. Persuading them will need a lot more effort in articulation.

What is the problem we are solving? How do we solve it? Garbled, unsculpted thoughts once chiselled down by the preciseness of speech become the first intangible in the creative process of growing a startup. The co-founder is the best collaborator for shaving down the rough exterior of the log. Long whiteboard sessions break down the thoughts, and the plans are now processed by several brains working in unison. Co-founders are allies who buy into the rough idea and are willing to give shape to it while living in uncertainty. No one knows at this stage whether any of this stuff makes sense. Its intuitive genesis gives no comfort of certainty. The process will go through multiple iterations and may require going back to square one more than once. Through each turn, the collaborative effort gets better and the time to definition gets faster. Now the problem statement is ready. Some founders see a breakthrough when they are able to explain their concept to people who are quite removed from their world. Like their parents or children. If this audience gets it, then the words are doing their job. Then there is no need to explain the answer.

After the problem statement is done, the founder will hire the early employees, work on the rational part of the plan, raise capital, and on achieving these milestones, they will formulate the irrational part of the plan and go about raising a larger round of capital.

Before the founder gets there, many more people will need to be convinced that funding and buying into the vision is the best choice they can make. The founder must persuade the early employees, the early investors and the early customers. The common word is 'early'.

The early employees. The brave, adventurous souls who thrive in uncertainty will be the first to try to make sense of the promise that the founder is trying to convince them of.

They want to believe as much as the founder wants to persuade. The founder has the highest ethos equity with this group.

Many of these employees are curious enough to force the best answer from the founder. 'What exactly do we do?' This question will be asked in interviews, at stand-ups and in restrooms. At times, the founder may be asked this question by the anxious parents of a young engineer who is veering away from the prescribed path of joining an MNC. Versions of this answer will float in the corridors until they become dangerously off from the original intent.

To bring all the employees on one page, the founder will write an email with the most precise business objective articulation to date. This email will be saved by many of the early employees and revisited when the company makes mega fundraising news several years later. The company will be very different from the one described in that email. As the mega founder pushes the goal forward, persuading people to believe in an expanding scale of ambition becomes more challenging. The larger the goal, the more difficult it is to believe, and the greater the convincing power needed to achieve it. The four key parts of this message are: Who we are, what we are trying to achieve, where we are and where we are going. The mega founder will rely on overcommunication. The message will be woven into emails, marketing, employee events, social media and presentations.

The fundraising pitch is the acid test of the founder's eloquence. The early investors point their guns in the direction of the wind. Despite being financial return-oriented investors, logos is not the only factor required to persuade them. Ethos and pathos are pivotal. Eventually, the founder's performance on this stage can be the make or break of a potential unicorn. Most investors will lean in or out within the first ten minutes of the pitch, irrespective of their cheque size. Many founders display passion and excitement but conveying the goal is hard because the goal definition is still in the rational plane. The rational goal is all logos. The irrational goal is dependent on ethos and it takes time to make it sound even half believable. Explaining it can drive the founder to use a lot of words, and before long, the pitch dissipates into mindless babble. I searched around the web and found that the word for this verbal diarrhoea is logorrhoea!

Eloquence deftly taken through the needle eye of simplicity needs to stitch the mess created by logorrhoea. The ability to convincingly convey the goal is an indicator of clarity of thought on what the business is capable of becoming. Simplicity combined with passion is a winning combination. Complexity combined with passion is a mess that makes the audience weary. For an investor, the founder's ability to communicate the business idea clearly is a corollary for clarity of thought. That clarity of thought indicates that the founding team has tested a lot of hypothetical business choices. The goal has been narrowed down from a host of choices. This in turn indicates that the team understands the customer and will build or has built the most appropriate solution. The same coherence of goal is believed to guide the team on a common mission with brutal execution focus.

Apple's first marketing brochure referred to simplicity as 'the ultimate sophistication'. With a lot going on in the founder's head, simplification is the hardest exercise.

I have seen thousands of pitches and the best ones are the simplest ones. They have narrowed down the problem and the solution to a level where a child could articulate it. A simple pitch sequences the chapters of a narrative into a single line of sight that when fired right between the investor's eyes will get them to follow up with interest. The best meetings are where the founder breaks a thirty-minute period into four chunks— five minutes to grab attention by explaining why the company is exciting, ten minutes to go in depth into the what and how, ten minutes to reinforce the claim of a large outcome, and the last five minutes to conclude the meeting on a high note.

What pieces of the business should the founder leave out in his pitch? How much of the work-in-progress is safe to convey as being 'done and dusted'? The investor is looking for these signals. A mega articulator picks out the extra bits until only the essential message is left. The founder has to carefully choose a style of speaking, ensuring that it is neither banal nor glib. For investors who listen to founders pitch several times a week, a style that is too safe can be sleep-inducing. On the other hand, by being glib, the founder will come across as shallow. Many founders use metaphors to convey complex ideas effectively. The Coinbase pitch deck has a slide that states that Coinbase is for Bitcoin what iTunes was for MP3.

Every investor is looking for the degree of conviction in a claim. Conviction also comes in uncomplicated packaging— drawn out into an arc from a small claim with proof to a bigger claim with proof and finally the biggest claim with no proof. The arc follows the believability curve and leaves the decision to the investor.

Speech is ineffective if it's not picking up as many cues from the silence of the listeners as it is from their questions. Reading the room is an acquired skill that is closely tied to watertight articulation. Some investor meetings can be so one-sided that the only voice in the meeting belongs to the founder. Valuable verbal and facial feedback is missed in the process. Conversely, over-engineered pitches fail to express conviction. The pliant message overshadows the uniqueness. Pitches can be memorable events for investors. It has been eighteen years and I still remember Vijay Shekhar Sharma's first pitch to me. His articulation skills were extraordinary even then and he could hold the room's attention with his speech.

Customers, especially the enterprise ones, are the no-bullshit audience who can severely cramp the founder's style. They leave little room for persuasion based on the founder's passion and excitement. In fact, that can have the reverse effect. The audience has no incentive to risk getting fired for taking a leap of faith with an unknown vendor. The founder has no big-brand customers to give comfort to the audience. It's a chicken-and-egg problem looking for a mama hen. Sometimes even the most eloquent founders fail in breaking this logjam and take the easy path of promising the moon. Projecting a larger-than-life image of the company, the founder sells a product that exists only on that office whiteboard. And agrees to a feature three months before the engineering team can deliver the product even if they were to slog night and day. Eloquence needs a tremendous amount of discernment. Choosing what needs to be promised within the realms of reality and what can be outside the realms of reality is the ultimate judgement call.

Most of us are trained to trust quantity over quality. Many founders struggle with practising minimalism when articulating important messages. They have a long list of things they want to talk about. They want to convey little bits about every topic on the list.

The list could include the purpose of the company, the value to the customer, the pricing, competitive moats being created, differentiation the capital needed, how the company will use the funds they raise, team strength and customer traction. Minimizing noise in messaging is hard work. The most important test is twofold—order of impact and narrative value. The highest impact items are obviously those that you want the listener to register and focus on. As easy as this sounds, many founders do not prioritize the list to two to three most impactful items relevant for that interaction.

Elimination and selection are at the heart of every strategic conversation. Any act of persuasion assumes that the listener has a choice. By prioritizing, we lower their cognitive choice load and make it easier for them to know what those choices are and how to select from them. If founders are making a hire, it won't help much to compare their startup with the faceless industry. The founder can compare the most likely startups that the hire could consider and list two reasons why they would be best off by joining their startup. Prioritizing also keeps the listeners motivated through the conversation. In a pitch deck, anything that talks about how big the opportunity is should be laid out upfront. In a customer meeting, it would make sense to talk about the benefits of the product before expounding on the strengths of the team. Mood-sensing is, of course, paramount. Founders who are good at picking up on facial cues sense any negativity in the room very quickly. They save the leap of faith ask until that negativity is reduced or eliminated. Founders who are great at persuasion also let investors, employees or customers feel in control of the decision. So while the ask is to invest, the founder never, never,

never asks the investor to invest. That decision is left open. Instead, they talk about the strengths and more-than-even chance of success of the venture. I know a founder who never ever says that the meeting is for a fundraise. Investors call back to check if the company is looking to raise more capital.

Investors, customers and potential employees are never under pressure to act but worry about missing out on the epic journey some lucky people are about to undertake.

Founders often come across new opportunities as they progress on the original one. There is pressure on them to focus resources on what is working and to ignore the 'distractions'. Moving the startup to focus on the next growth opportunity is a cause of worry for the shareholders and is not encouraged. Many such growth initiatives can remain bullet points on board meeting presentations without ever getting acted on.

A mega founder will always look to build upon multiple market flywheels in the course of building a company. Amazon, Google and Facebook never stopped building new flywheels, and in the process, they found ways to generate multiple revenue streams starting from a single thread of customer success. Two flywheels firing together can multiply the size of the business many times over. Not only is the original value proposition delivered but it has been supplemented in the form of revenue growth and valuation increase. The complexity of explaining the vision also rises exponentially as conviction takes root in an emerging flywheel. Shepherding a startup from a product to a platform with multiple products involves the risk of losing the original value. It's always double or quits for startups who choose to chase flywheels. Persuading the naysayers about the vision can be a daunting stepping stone.

Flywheels can be kept hidden from public scrutiny until their potential for success is demonstrable. Only the inner circle is aware of the attractive adjoining opportunities the founder is considering. To gather some real-life examples, I visited a founder's house for a chat. It was a Sunday afternoon and the house was packed with relatives visiting from his hometown. The kitchen was operating at maximum capacity and had just produced a fresh batch of Kanpur-style samosas. I would have liked to savour the rich brown imli chutney drizzled over the samosa more mindfully but the topic of flywheels and their pursuit had to be attended to with full attention. After one bite of the flaky skin, I settled back to listen to what was a successful level-up.

The founder shared that he had a hard time convincing his board to take a leap into the new flywheel. A related opportunity that could add $100 billion in value to the current best case of $10 billion was unproven and a big risk. This was despite the fairest path offered to investors for value creation—offering the existing shareholders the same ownership in the new venture as the current business. The shareholders were not ready to bite because they felt that the $10 billion venture was by itself so large and valuable that there was no obvious incentive to risk it by chasing potential shadows. The founder started work on the new flywheel in a low-key manner, treating it like a kitchen-sink experiment. As it picked up pace, it became a more prominent update in the investor conversations. Once its viability became more obvious, it was brought into prime-time discussion and drew some real fund allocation. The new flywheel is now as big a valuation driver as the original business and has a revenue potential that is far bigger as well. The samosa was a painful sacrifice to understand how stakes around the founder's power of persuasion get bigger even after initial success is achieved.

Bud Tribble, a member of the original Macintosh development team at Apple, coined the term 'reality distortion field'. He cofounded NeXT with Steve Jobs and is now one of the three policy czars at Apple for privacy. Bud observed the spell that Steve Jobs cast on the Mac development team, convincing them to set their goals at unrealistic levels. Lo and behold, the team delivered on many of the goals that had been called preposterous. It is said that Bud came up with this term after seeing a *Star Trek* episode called 'Menagerie' in which the aliens created a new world using their mental force. He found that under Steve's power of speech, 'reality is malleable' because he could 'convince anyone of practically anything'.[*]

In the words of Andy Hertzfeld who reported to Bud, 'The reality distortion field was a confounding melange of

---

[*] Walter Isaacson, *Steve Jobs* (Abacus, 2015).

a charismatic rhetorical style, an indomitable will, and an eagerness to bend any fact to fit the purpose at hand. If one line of argument failed to persuade, he would deftly switch to another. Sometimes, he would throw you off balance by suddenly adopting your position as his own, without acknowledging that he ever thought differently."*

Since it was attributed to the legendary Steve Jobs, the concept has been glorified to the point that its damaging aspect is often ignored. Reality distortion is the art of persuading an incredulous person through forceful speech to believe in something implausible.

A person's willingness to buy into the founder's claim is dependent on a lack of information about the difficulties involved and their natural tendency to resolve the cognitive dissonance that arises when the argument contradicts their existing beliefs. How much liberty should a founder take when differentiating between the work in progress, the real and the plan? Because when everything is spoken and nothing is checked, what prevents a founder from presenting claimed progress as real?

Like any strength, reality distortion once discovered will be used over and over again as a potent solution for achieving impossible deadlines. Using it indiscriminately could cause a higher rate of team burnout, and if the goals are frequently missed, it will damage the founder's credibility. Pushing it

---

* Source: Folklore.org: Reality Distortion Field website

beyond reason to wilfully fool people will result in failure. I once came close to giving a term sheet to a software-as-a-service business whose founder claimed a $100,000 annual recurring revenue that would grow to $1 million in the next six months based on contracts. The claim was exciting as it pointed to many customers adopting a unique and reasonably high-priced product. On talking to the customers, however, it became clear that what was presented as contracted revenue was actually trials with a possibility of being converted into contracted long-term recurring revenue. In presenting the product's traction, the founder had chosen words that clearly distorted the facts. Theranos and WeWork are dark examples of how the gap between real and unreal can become blurry beyond a point.

A founder will have three kinds of people to convince. The first will naturally look up to them and will anchor around the narrative coming from the founder. They buy into the founder's vision. Aristotle would say this persuasion uses pathos by appealing to the emotions of the audience. This set of people continues to follow the founder despite errors in the vision itself as long as they are kept in the loop. Communicating with them needs the least persuasion. If the vision needs course correction, the founder makes sure that he conveys it to this set first. Founders make sure that they treat their trust as sacrosanct. As long as trust is maintained, they will continue to complete the founder's sentences and strive to achieve.

The second set of people are those who go not by narrative but by metrics. They need details and believe something only when they see it. Leaving the communication at vision level will be lost on this group. Out of the 100 micro steps needed to execute the vision, the founder must have taken five steps to convince this lot. If the execution is failing, the founder will make sure that this lot understands why. Aristotle would say the founder would deploy logos in order to persuade this set.

For both groups, a founder's ability to communicate includes an openness to admitting failure. Explaining failure and admitting confusion are not seen as signs of weakness by either group. A founder's attempt to camouflage failure with bravado is picked up by these groups and leads to loss of faith. Mega founders are aware that the people around them do not expect them to be right all the time. This vulnerability creates long-lasting trust and nudges people to step forward to help the founder.

The third set exists outside the startup. These are the investors, media, influencers and industry commentators who are observing the founder from a distance; their access is limited to the electronic media's bite-sized version of the world—over-indexing on capturing attention. The founder's ethos is paramount for this set. This group is best communicated with by anchoring the vision to an idea that is already present in the real world. A successful anchoring will lead to startups in their early stages being referred to as the Uber of long haul, the OYO of hospitals or the Instagram of religion.

Like all things in life, there will be naysayers here as well. A founder is not going to win 100 per cent support from everyone. Accepting this and not sweating over the 5 per cent of naysayers helps to keep things moving along.

Eloquence is a necessary ingredient to create new worlds and is essential for mega outcomes. Communicating effectively requires judgement, self-awareness, empathy and openness. It is a powerful tool to convey complex ideas, blurry visions and early signs of execution. It places the burden of credibility on the founder. While the arm-waving and passion are well accepted, the onus is on the founder to sustain and build upon the credibility that was accorded to them based on their past achievements. While unwavering confidence is important to build followership, it can easily cause stress in the founder to maintain the facade even when the train is going off the tracks due to faulty vision or execution. Honesty and trust are ideal companions to eloquence. Mega founders remain genuinely vulnerable as they set their sights on the next flywheel of opportunity.

6

Marathon Mindset

'As you set out for Ithaka
hope your road is a long one.
Full of adventure, full of discovery.
Laestrygonians, Cyclopes and angry Poseidon,
don't be afraid of them.'

—Constantine P. Cavafy

For anyone who has run or attempted to run even a half-marathon, it takes just a few hours to realize that the gruelling endurance test is more of the mind than the body. The body under the command of a resolute mind can limp and hobble to the finish line despite cramps and blisters. On the mind's ability to overcome, the four-minute-mile ceiling breaker, Roger Bannister, said, 'The body achieves what the mind believes.' In Indian philosophy, there is a sophisticated analysis of the nature of the mind as a manifestation of the brain. The mind is considered to be naturally turbulent, but with practice and detachment, it can be controlled. The runner's mind is chaotic to begin with. It notices all the aches, the itching and the dampness of the sweat troubling the body. Runners embrace these discomforts as inevitable and accept them, but after running a particular distance, these distractions are no longer observable. The mind goes into a zone, melting the sun-scorched world into blurry, unfocused images in the peripheral vision. As the brain optimizes oxygen allocation to the most important cells, the runner loses the ability to process the rush-hour traffic of thoughts.

As a VC who has taken the ride with multiple founders on a decade-long company-growing journey, I find the marathon runner analogy to be uncannily apt. The long and arduous journey of a startup can be paced better using principles for a well-planned and well-run marathon.

Japanese writer Haruki Murakami says, 'I run in a void. Or maybe I should put it the other way: I run in order to acquire a void.'* This void makes the body place one foot in front of the other until the finish line is crossed. The foot lifts effortlessly and lands just as the other rises. The training is essential but on the day of the run, a runner relies on carbohydrate loading, race nutrition, mental prompting and pacing. One of the most common visualizations a marathon runner uses is breaking down the forty-two kilometres into smaller chunks. The mind rewards itself by achieving smaller goals and does not get overwhelmed by the length of the run. Another powerful

---

* Haruki Murakami, *What I Talk About When I Talk About Running* (Knopf Doubleday Publishing Group, 2009).

technique, called kinaesthetic imagery, uses the mental eye to imagine the muscles involved in a movement contracting and expanding. Cross-country runners visualize the entire course down to the last detail including its inclines and declines, the angle of the sun, the smell of the trees, where they would surge or conserve energy and for how long.

Seasoned marathon runner Eliud Kipchoge was raised by a single mom on a farm in a remote Kenyan village called Kapsisiywa. Located in the Kenyan Highlands, Kapsisiywa is as remote as remote gets. Eliud would run on the red dusty roads, back and forth from school, then go around on his cycle delivering newspapers and milk. He saved money for five months before he could buy his first pair of running shoes. When he met his lifelong coach Patrick Sang for the first time, Patrick shared a regimen that he wanted Eliud to follow. Eliud didn't have anything to write it on, so he scratched it on his skin with a twig.

Patrick's lifelong philosophy is that athletes should try to understand themselves, work at their maximum potential and unabashedly seek information from anybody, any expert who can help them grow as an athlete. He feels that each person's potential is completely different from the next person's, so the important thing is to work on one's own capability.

Marathoners like Eliud carefully plan their energy expenditure to maximize performance. Despite breaking the two-hour full marathon time barrier in Austria, he self-critiqued his choice of pace in the run. He regretted his decision to run a flat two hours instead of running the planned 60:40 pace. Eliud did not run at a slower pace for the first 60 per cent and felt that 'he went too fast' and that took 'energy from the muscles'. The acceptance of the finite limitation of the human body is baked into the core of planning a winning race. The finite energy and strength have to be stretched over the length of the race such that they are sustained and available when most required. Rush early, slow later. Slow now, rush later. Pace in a marathon is determined by the demand that the terrain will place on your muscles. Anticipating the incline and decline and planning the dispensing of strength is the pacing required in a marathon. Knowing that the searing pain in the twelfth kilometre has to be tolerated for another thirty kilometres is pacing the marathon. When we focus on the pacing, we are letting process take over. The outcome of breaking the barrier is less important than planning the use of the finite amount of energy.

We are trained from childhood to pace our activities to ensure a successful outcome within finite resources. Finiteness is the biggest teacher of this principle. In the India of the 1970s and 1980s, before hot water in faucets became ubiquitous, a hot bath meant using wood or the more expensive LPG to heat water. At my home in Dehradun, on cold winter mornings, water was heated in a large vessel, and a finite quantity was given to every member of the family to use as judiciously as they could. You could choose to lower the temperature of the mix by adding more cold water, but the quantity was the trade-off between a bucket of lukewarm water or a nicely steaming half bucket of water. Recognition of this choice and the finiteness of resources helps instil the need to pace. When we eat an Indian meal, the chapatis need to keep pace with the vegetables and dal. There is no fun in chewing on dry chapatis by themselves, so we pace the portion of vegetables and dal that we have in every morsel. We learn this skill from the time we take over the responsibility of sustaining ourselves, but when it comes to growing startups, many founders can't keep a measured pace in the build. They run out of cash, build unwieldly organizations, burn relationships, lose credibility, over-dilute their equity and create more stress than necessary for everyone around them.

As a board member and an engaged observer of the journey, the view I am fortunate to have is the long arc of time stretching from the start of the idea to the point it becomes a cashflow-positive company. This arc stretches a length of time that allows for the creation of deep relationships among people from the same and opposing quarters. The long time frames are not forgiving to short-term thinking. Choosing the right people and keeping them around is a strong determinant of success. They will help you weather the inevitable storms that will come repeatedly over this long arc.

These relationships have to last two decades or more. In this time, they will be tested by distrust, the frequent near shutdown of the business, new faces in the leadership team, new board members, new revenue lines, customer departures, pivots, new flywheels . . . so both the length of the journey and the many pressures have to be kept in mind. The founder's journey could stretch over ten to twelve years. In that period, on the personal front, a founder who began their journey in their late twenties would possibly get married, have children, slow down physically, spend more time with ageing parents and become aware of their own mortality. Co-founders and colleagues could leave, start, build and make their millions at other startups. There is pressure to stay on top of a constantly changing environment and there is fear of finding their competition being replaced by the new startup founders—who are as young and brash as when they started. Personal constraints add up with every passing year. Personal growth is seriously hampered if the founder does not see this journey for its length, and with the home front becoming more complex than three bachelors cranking code in an apartment, the inability to handle it well will cause a downward spiral in energy and ability to build further. The seam can unravel very fast and the recovery can take years.

Maturity from life's lessons should accrue to the sensible founder. As founders realize the humanness in their super humanness, they grow. The responsibility for carrying the feelings and emotions of people at home as well as of their team leaders will dawn on them. They will touch the lives of others around them. The collective lifting of this group's aspirations and maturity is the only way to keep pace with the demands of a startup as it ages.

If founders were to dwell upon the compressed periods of stress that they are experiencing, they would feel disheartened and discouraged. Thankfully, founders don't overanalyse the past. Their ability to focus on the future keeps them sane. They chug along as changes unfold. The mind is in the zone of creating and surviving. They remember that the journey is long.

Just like in a marathon, pace management is the code for running startups too. Those who don't pace themselves will suffer from more cramping and muscle fatigue than others. Those who don't visualize the distance in smaller segments may find themselves mentally overwhelmed and unable to deal with the stress. Pressure can cause burnout. Flywheel after flywheel will appear but the founder's energy will be so spent that they will not be able to seize them. Thousands of startups start well. They power out of the starting gate with the energy of the promise. The initial demand on the startup is to prove themselves. They plan a rational goal, slog and achieve it. That is a win in a young startup. Then the startup moves forward on the path of the irrational goal. As it ages, it has to switch from proving itself to defending itself. As it builds revenue streams and grows customers, it demands strength from the entire body to handle the rigours of the marathon.

If the founder does not chart out the journey, they will continue to focus on the same muscles that got them started, even as the startup ages. A startup could end up having a strong product team, which is what got it the initial breakthrough, but if other important teams are not developed, then the imbalance starts to weigh down its fighting ability in the face of a threat. Weak muscles, such as financial control or human resources, which are not strengthened come under strain and eventually collapse because they just cannot cope with performing at higher thresholds.

As headcount rises, the weight of hiring and churning, training and managing starts to hold back the startup's momentum. Mega founders see this as an obvious demand on the body and pace themselves according to the new running conditions. They become very focused on their human resource management function. They bring in strategic HR leaders and put together a function that balances the leadership skills to better run that part of the organization that goes beyond the founding team. Leaders who struggle to manage larger teams are replaced with those who have experience in running organizations. This reduces the painful headache that occurs predictably in years four and five of the journey and is responsible for hampering the scale-up process.

Mega founders train for the marathon but run it like a sprint. Let us not confuse a startup's journey with the speed of a marathon. Investors love faster return on the capital they have put into a startup. India is unique in the lack of appreciation for the opportunity cost of growing startups. Many investors have not seen an exit from their ten-year-old investment in startups. When asked how long they have been waiting, they let out exasperated groans. If the founder comes to work every day thinking that their build time is ten to fifteen years, then they will miss many of the rewards that come with speed. And there is a good chance that the outcome won't be attractive in size. A marathon mindset is the appreciation that the business is being built to last long so every brick needs to fit snugly. The marathon mindset helps prevent burnout and reduces the baggage load of a startup.

A marathon mindset founder's personal growth happens faster than the startup. As the startup ages, the founder's rate of maturity outstrips it. When a founder thinks long term about the foundation of the startup, they look for repeatability and solidity. Practices are repeatable and solid when they fit a set of 'values'. Founders need to define the values they want the people in the startup to anchor around. Values are like goals—once published, they promote adherence because everyone who reads them does a good job comparing reality versus myth. Values are standard words like integrity, collaboration, passion.

They are simple but they put a line in the sand on what the founders expect from their employees. Values have to be demonstrated, explained and reiterated.

Founders need to know their mind when it comes to defining the values that they want to run the organization by. This old-world practice is often ignored until consultants drag the founders crying and screaming back to the whiteboard and force them to cough up superfluous words. This jargon-generating exercise sounds hokey because it is not done honestly enough. Founders are not honest because they do not know their own mind. They have never sat down to think deeply about what drives them and what impact they want their company to have on the world. Up until now the adrenaline has kept the founder running. They have had no time to pause and contemplate the world they are creating. What would it look like, what kind of people would live there, what language would they speak?

Remember Maruti Uncle? He created a burning fire in the founder to go prove himself. All founders carry their baggage and are not inherently sorted-out human beings to grow companies with thousands of employees. They jump into the fire with the confidence of being doers and achievers. Tremendous confidence is required to make a life mission around an idea. To sustain this confidence, founders need to put on blinders to their flaws. These blinders help the founders attain critical velocity, but then like rockets that jettison their spent fuel tanks after reaching zero gravity, these blinders need to fall off.

These blinders on capability gaps obstruct the growth of both the founder and the startup. Self-discovery removes these blinders, and mega founders choose to proactively get their shit together before the myopia starts holding them back. Self-discovery can come out of a quiet meditative session, but most of us don't listen to that little voice in our head. We need real people around us to tell us what our blind spots are. Founders can receive feedback from their co-founders, employees and spouses. Not many founders seek feedback in a formal manner. Not much good comes of feedback that is not sought earnestly. As a board member, I do not waste my breath giving unsolicited feedback, but rather use my energy to get the founder to a place where they seek answers to why the startup is stalling, why their leadership team keeps churning, why their big funding round is elusive, or why their co-founders are ready to quit. Some issues are fixable with time, but some will cause permanent damage, like a co-founder departure. Board members wince when they see the founder running at breakneck speed towards the well of common founder mistakes. An ego pumped by big valuations and generous cash-outs does not make for an easy listener. Openness to feedback is a raw experience in shattering the ego. This ego has been providing the most soothing balm to the flesh wound left by Maruti Uncle. Ego removal is necessary for feedback to work, but it comes with pain. To achieve mega status, founders must recognize the inevitability of hitting the wall before permanent damage sets in. An awake founder's mind accepts the pain of fallibility and perceived loss of face in self-improvement.

From being engrossed with their self-image of 'Mr Has All the Answers', 'visionary' and 'has tremendous clarity', the founder sheds such monikers and accepts that on some aspects of building, they haven't the faintest clue. This shedding causes pain. But this pain is very rewarding. Mega founders manage to overcome this pain in return for the reward that feedback and growth will bring. This painful, introspective exercise has furthered the longevity of many well-known startups. The founder realizes that their confidence does not go away. It stays strong and has faith and awareness as compared to chaotic energy.

Only when a founder has a marathon mindset will he value the delayed gratification of hitting scale and catching multiple flywheels vis-à-vis the pain of self-improvement.

What do successful founders discover and what do they grow into? They discover the power of managing growth versus powering through it. They grow into scale leaders who can blend their growth style with a management style. This is the only way to bring in professional leaders who will lead the broader contours that the startup has now acquired. The multiple moving parts can be handed off to professionals who are trained to handle the complexity.

Founders can now go back to spending time on their true passion and first love—their customers and employees.

By focusing on them, the founder will once again give the required attention to the two most vital parts of the equation. In the beginning, quick customer wins are good enough to set the momentum. In reality, though, the customers are short-changed. The early employees are underpaid and over-promised. Once they have transformed to scale leaders, founders discover that there is tremendous headroom in customer delight. They go back to the core and create products that fail less and are easier to use. On the back end of this, the startup discovers network effects, which they can now pass on as higher value for the customer—book cabs anywhere with an app, order any kind of cab, order for any kind of need and expect the same superior customer experience. When customers rave about their experience, the founder discovers greater purpose in this feedback. This purpose feeds into the marathon mindset.

Employees are loyal to the founder partly because they believe in them but also because they expect outsized rewards to justify the opportunity cost and insecurity that their spouses remind them of every day. As founders overcome their own vulnerability in favour of a growth mindset, they invest more emotional energy into their team by empowering them to accept the growth path mindset. Building for the long term requires treating people like humans. If in the rush to build there is a pile of bodies collecting on the side of the road, it's time to reflect on the long-term implications.

Not respecting commitments to employees may seem like a one-time event but there is always a pattern to this. Founders may ignore it but the trust deficit builds up quickly. It knocks off the zeal from employee motivation.

Not fulfilling a verbal but undocumented commitment on stock options may feel all right but it is unfair for those who were made to believe in this carrot that never appeared. Seldom will a marathon mindset founder take a nice payoff for himself by selling their equity in an investment transaction while leaving the stock option holders to find liquidity in the distant IPO. Founders who undertake the pain of meeting every employee who is being let go to conserve cash show a mega founder trait. They communicate to the employees that their well-laid-out plans went awry and the startup needs to be saved by cutting HR costs. This open-heart exercise involves enduring short-term pain for the long-term setting of a culture that cares about its employees. Founders rely on their strength to admit failure and their eloquence to convey coherently why they need to take hard decisions for the long-term success of the company. These employees learn the most important lesson that a successful founder can teach—to seek self-growth despite the pain of chipping away at the ego. Founders with a marathon mindset recognize contributions from the team and set up reward systems that are broad and fair.

A journey of self-discovery has the side effect of opening many closed doors for the founders. They can meet some of their ghosts, shake hands and resolve some pending arguments. This could lead to them discovering love for themselves as humans. They can recognize the special gift they have to create lasting value for society.

By opening the doors to honest introspection and some ego manhandling, a Key becomes a mega founder. With all this universal love filling their lives, founders grow into more positive, happier and healthier versions of themselves. They receive more trust from their teams, their spouses and their children, and this gives them more strength to dial up their goals. The loneliness of being a solitary builder gives way to more connectedness. Only a rare founder would not feel demotivated by the gnawing thought that their children are growing up without them spending enough time in their lives. When they continue to receive the affirmation of being a good spouse, a good parent, a good leader, they can take on more demanding paths of building mega startups.

In the long journey of growing a startup, a founder without a marathon mindset loses perspective under pressure. Funding gets delayed. A banker brings in a lowball offer of acquisition and the founder starts to actively consider selling because they feel that this offer is more attractive than it actually is, just because the chips are down. The swing to negativity is extreme. To the founder, it feels like the ship is about to sink, and the offer has come as a lifeline. The power to reverse the swing to the optimistic zone depends on some elusive investor who is expected to appear magically to invest in the startup.

This swing to extreme negativity happens when, amidst the pressure and lack of options, the founder takes a microscopic view of the journey. They discount the value they have created and forget all the odds they overcame to get here. In such situations, someone should remind the founder to switch to the telescope view—they should realize that this 'dire situation' will appear as a blip in the long arc of ten years. The value that will be created at the end of that long arc will be so large that it will dwarf any calamity. It is worth reassessing the cost of dealing with it and negotiating from a position of strength. If the long-term value is not visible to the founder through a telescope, then it's better to take the lowball offer and run as fast as possible with the consideration paid out in as much cash as possible. A focus on the perspective of long-term value creation rather than on the multiple calamities that show up along the way is a true reflection of a marathon mindset.

Opportunity cost is a counter view to this keep-building approach. Why not move out consciously from a startup if it's not working out? Why bother running the full marathon? For one, in India, the opportunities require extra-long builds because they are not capitalizing on technology shifts but on white space, tech-enabled new business creation. Bailing out may be a premature decision in hindsight.

All fast-moving startups cause mental strain to the builders with their wildly oscillating fortunes. Tremendous mental strength is needed to barrel through so much uncertainty. The founder must have an optimistic streak so they can see every day as day one. A startup grown by a founder with the marathon mindset will grow on top of a solid foundation, treat its customers with care, investors and employees with respect, have fundamental profitability in its business model and will not stop becoming more valuable than yesterday, every day. It does not chase indiscriminate user growth without first having a handle on their propensity to convert to real paying customers. It does not grow without learning why and what is growing. It bakes fast learning loops into its DNA to receive feedback on where it can improve. And it never ever loses touch with the value it is creating for its customers.

7

Mitochondria

'All phenomena are processes, connections, all is in flux . . .
have the mind screens knocked away to see there is no real
edge to anything, that in the endless interpenetration of the
universe, a molecular flow, a cosmic energy shimmers in all
stone and steel as well as flesh . . .'

—Peter Matthiessen, *The Snow Leopard*

Founders work hard. I know of several for whom the day ends
well past midnight. Yet the next morning, they are ready to
conquer the world. They do not come into the office with
droopy eyes and long yawns. As soon as the day starts, they
light up their teams to go and seize the day. Every meeting,
every corridor conversation and town hall has the same energy
level. The founder is vibrating at the same frequency as on day
one. This infectious energy installs the armour of invincibility
in every team member.

When I walk into a high-energy startup office it has the
same physiological effect on my senses that watching a live

music concert or a cricket match does. It is not the noise but the resonance of the crowd with the performers. There is an electric buzz in the air that this resonance generates. The crowd is fully invested in the success of the performance, remains ultra-focused on every nuance and is emotionally connected to the outcome.

A founder's unwavering energy flow is a rare advantage that is available only to startups. Founders are human dynamos who generate enough energy for the entire team. They fire up their team to raise their performance to ten times their potential. The team, when hooked up to their supercharger, is galvanized to achieve the unthinkable. Fuelled up on energy through funding winters, elusive paying customers or widely publicized layoffs, the founder remains in high-performance mode through every adversity.

To understand the flow of energy or the life force, 'prana', a startup has to be seen for what it really is. It is born and it grows. The birth of a startup on day zero adds creative energy to the universe. It is its big bang moment. This is the moment when the founder made up their mind to dedicate all their energy to the materialization of their idea. The elements present at the big bang moment continue through the process of growing. Growing from the inside out, a startup resembles a germinating seed or a flower turning into a fruit. Energy suffusing the being of the startup enables the various parts to grow sequentially, eventually making the whole come together.

It is not an object being put together piecemeal but a body building up from within. It starts from the same building block as a living body at birth with the 'totipotent' zygote— that one cell that will rapidly multiply into differentiated cells, each cell finding its purpose to perform specialized functions. As Alan Watts puts it[*], 'Growing and making are entirely different procedures.' He says that 'when you make something, you put it together—you arrange it in parts, you work from outside to the in. That's how a potter works on clay, or a sculptor works on stone'. When something grows, 'it happens in the opposite direction—that is from inside to the out'.

In this living organism, functional groups such as product and engineering are like the organs, doing their specific functions but dependent on a centralized, intelligently orchestrated energy flow. The founder converts fuel into energy, which permeates through the body, allowing the cells to develop and perform. Like the critical source of prana in the human body, the founder has to be efficient in the conversion of fuel to energy, agnostic to the fuel type available and aware of every organ's needs at all times. With so many dependencies, the source of the vital life force cannot afford to take even a minute off. The founder is omnipresent with a touch point to all teams. They are the most aware entity in a startup, the

---

[*] Alan Watts, *Out of Your Mind: Tricksters, Interdependence and the Cosmic Game of Hide-and-Seek* (Souvenir Press, 2019).

best informed to balance priorities and needs. They energize product and engineering teams in build phases and power up the sales team in the revenue phase.

They consume all types of fuel every day—work hours, capital, ideas, customer feedback, negativity, losing out to competition, investor rejection and inspiration from other companies. The founder can metabolize this diet most efficiently by insulating the startup from negativity and squeezing out energy even from a rejection.

Energy will flow both to tasks that are predictable and to dealing with surprises. Not a day will pass without a shock to the system. Prioritizing the flow of energy is a dynamic process dependent on internal and external surprises. The founder has to choose their daily battles and energize the parts of the startup that need to respond to threats and those that need to keep building in peace.

When a founder comes to work, these threats are waiting for them like angry pups, barking, whining and biting. These angry pups need to be carried to the finish line without being dropped.

Some founders do not keep in mind that their energy needs careful rationing. It cannot be monopolized by one of these pups. Nor can they remain in self-congratulatory bliss between each pup. They cannot be thrilled about minor accomplishments or remain over-engaged with just the parts of the business that are their natural strength.

I have observed that founders can have widely varying senses of the magnitude of their accomplishment. Some portray it as one of many while others make it sound as if 90 per cent of the energy in the system was used up to overcome this one thing.

Founders who cannot keep the energy flowing are unable to simultaneously move multiple pups forward to the finish line. These founders take on one task and become hyper-focused on it. They are consumed with the pup that has the loudest bark and only with its movement forward. After placing it at the next milepost, they scan the environment to determine their next high priority task. But by that time, it may already be too late for some priorities. They go back to where the other priority pups sit waiting for someone to move them forward. Priorities made to wait are not happy things to deal with. They are angry and they are starting to bite. These founders finally make up their mind, pick up the next pup and carry it forward while enduring the small agonizing bites. They find themselves constantly occupied yet everyone around them finds them to be unavailable. The cycle of busyness is vicious and never-ending. Their bandwidth remains scarce and exhaustion sets in early. Chronically busy founders are slow to respond to introductions made by board members and even their own employees have to wait for days to hear back from them.

A mega founder has infinite bandwidth. They handle multiple priorities together and don't waste time figuring out what next every time one pup is dealt with. They prefer carrying a handful of angry pups in their arms because they do not want to go back to even more viciousness. The Key avoids the angry bites and remains in a high-energy state. They grab the pups, run fast and hand them off to different owners as quickly as they can. In this way, all priority items get completed in their time windows. The Key's suggested approach to problems is what the team waits for, not for him to actually handle everything to closure. It's the rapidity of a suggested path forward and hand-offs that keep things moving forward in Key-led startups. Energy is transmitted to more functions at the same time and the Key's availability frees up faster.

One of the startups that I am on the board of ran into a tight situation where the founder had many demands on the business, all of which needed to be fulfilled as quickly as possible. Their biggest problem was that the cash in their bank account allowed them a maximum runway of twelve months. They had to raise fresh capital fast. This entailed finalizing a fund-raising pitch, then reaching out to and pitching to a long list of investors. Meanwhile, their cash was depleting fast, and their largest spend was on acquiring new customers. Marketing experiments were unproven and they didn't know which ones were going to work. Every successive month of marketing spend was adding to the burn. Some investors felt that they should slow down growth and focus on reducing their burn. They also needed to make two critical hires—a product manager and a growth leader. The product manager would support growth by increasing the effectiveness of marketing spend. The growth lead would hyper-focus on the marketing experiments to pick and scale the effective ones.

So, the priorities for the founder were:

1. Extend the runway in an uncertain funding environment.
2. Understand what's working in marketing and extract more efficiency from the spend.
3. Make the two hires and get them to hit the low-hanging fruit.
4. Get the pitch ready. Allow the business to continue growing at an exciting level so new investors would appreciate the potential. The pitch needed to go out in thirty days. The message had to be crafted and finalized. Investor meetings had to be set up.

The founder worked on all these priorities simultaneously because none of them could wait. All the issues were related and impacted the near-term growth choice. If the founder tackled them one by one, the startup would come under capital pressure and fall into a downward spiral of low growth, no new hires to focus on growth and no new funding.

The marketing cost was cut down by a quarter. Despite that, the team managed to eke out enough juice from the lowered marketing spend to keep new-user acquisitions on track. This freed up enough cash to make the two crucial hires. The new deck had an impressive growth plan with an acquisition cost that was lower than before. By the time the funding came in, the growth and product managers had joined the team and could perform their roles in a well-funded startup. Throughout this period, the founder was charged up to take on more priorities.

Startups are living beings. They will grow. They will get tired. They will put on fat. They will age. They may also suffer chronic stress. They need to sustain themselves through numerous high-energy-burst events. Energy consumption could be balanced, spiky or underutilized.

Startup metabolization rates are make or break for success. To perform at its peak, a startup must metabolize efficiently. In this state, it will move fast and do more. It will remain competitive and manage a day-one mindset even years after the big bang. How does a startup metabolize efficiently and continue to maintain the youthful rate of metabolism? How do humans metabolize efficiently? An article titled 'The Truth about Metabolism' published by Harvard Health Publishing defines metabolism as 'the internal process by which your body expends energy and burns calories. It runs 24/7 to keep your body moving, even when you're resting or sleeping, by converting the food and nutrients you consume into the energy your body needs in order to breathe, circulate blood, grow and repair cells, and everything else it does to survive'.

To understand metabolism, we have to take a peek into the complex process of energy generation in our cells. Evolving from single-cell organisms, life on earth has developed into a diverse set of living creatures, most of whom resemble each other in the way their bodies produce the energy to survive. The chemistry of metabolism is simply that of converting food energy into chemical energy. All the action takes place in the cells where glucose and oxygen are converted into energy. Three interrelated pathways—the Krebs cycle, electron transfer and glycolysis—create energy. Ninety per cent of this energy is dependent on a minicell that is believed to have descended from an ancient bacterium and is now present inside most human cells. This is the mitochondria, the powerhouse of cells.

Those who eat chicken know that certain parts of the bird consist of dark meat while others contain white meat, also called slow twitch and fast twitch fibres. Fast twitch fibres are used in activities like sprints in which energy is used up in a very short period of time (chicken breast please, I'm watching my cholesterol). Slow twitch fibres need to perform over long periods of time and are the dark meat muscles (chicken legs, anyone?). They are dark because they are packed with mitochondria.

Hans Adolf Kreb, after whom the Krebs cycle is named, is credited with establishing the sequence of chemical reactions involved in cellular respiration. In the Krebs cycle, acetyl-CoA, a molecule present in the food we eat, is broken down into carbon dioxide and water. This breakdown sets into motion a battery-like action. In his book *Transformer,*[*] Nick Lane compares the mitochondria to a battery charger releasing a charge across the cell membrane. Protons ejected from the cell force their way back through the cell membrane by rotating a turbine-like entrance. This 'bolt of lightning' creates the universal unit of energy in the form of a molecule called ATP. ATP releases its energy to power everything—from the electric charge in neurons in the brain to powering the filters in the kidney. From the chaotic distribution of calories in the food we eat, the body brings order by releasing energy in units of ATP.

Nobel Prize-winning Hungarian chemist Albert Szent-Györgyi was the first to observe the Krebs cycle in a lab and is credited with saying that life is nothing but an electron looking for a place to rest. An excited electron, rotating not too close around the nucleus, needs just enough energy from an external source to pass on to another atom. Once acquired by the new atom, it assumes a relaxed state and releases its energy. At the core of every change is a transfer of energy when a system moves from a high state of excitation to a lower one. A founder acts like the mitochondria for the startup—present in every cell, hyper-metabolizing units of ATP from their chaotic diet of disappointments, inspirations and never-say-die attitude. Their own state of excitation comes to rest when they have

---

[*] Nick Lane, *Transformer: The Deep Chemistry of Life and Death* (WW Norton & Company, 2022).

discharged a bolt of electricity into different parts of the startup. As energy flows, new cells are generated, organs develop and cells communicate with each other.

The tiny hummingbird has the highest metabolic rate in the animal kingdom. Although tiny, the high-speed fluttering of their wings can carry hummingbirds over 500 miles in a single night, hitting top speeds of 33 miles per hour. Their wings beat 5400 times a minute when hovering. Comparatively, the fans on a CFM56 engine, like the ones installed on Boeing 737 aircraft, rotate 3200 times a minute.

A hummingbird can generate such a huge quantum of energy because they siphon the most efficient fuel available in flowers—pure glucose in the form of nectar. For a founder, the best nectar is the clarity of their execution plan. A plan that breaks the journey into small parts and nails down the precise levers and milestones to level to the next phase. Who am I trying to hire, who am I selling to, what am I selling, what should the product be achieving, how much money do I have for this phase, and who is responsible for achieving what in the team? A founder can achieve a lot in a day when they know precisely who to follow up with, what questions to ask, what input to reiterate and what to kick off.

Purity of purpose and single-mindedness to achieve it raises the founder's ability to metabolize more efficiently. Purity of purpose is based on the right intent. Free from impurities like making unfounded claims, lack of self-belief or recurring incongruence in the founding team, a founder's purity of purpose can provide them with the glucose-like fuel to metabolize like a hummingbird. Single-minded pursuit can make this fuel even more potent. It requires the founder to cut off lifelines that budget for Plan Bs—by considering that Plan A could fail. There is no turning back once this happens. A founder hedging the odds of success by factoring for failure or being stuck in the chicken-and-egg cycle that growth won't come until funding and funding won't come until growth happens will remain on the precipice, balancing between the worlds of should and could.

Moby Dick is a book about a crew that sets off on a quest on board a whaling ship called the *Pequod* to catch an elusive whale called Moby Dick. Whaling was a risky endeavour that brought windfall profits to the crew and the financiers but required a strong stomach for risk. In a climactic moment in the book, the *Pequod* is caught in a typhoon and the despairing crew is ready to give up on it and themselves. Just then, in a grand display of conviction, the captain of the *Pequod* not only stands on the deck with steadfast resolution but also ties himself to the mast. Inspired by this sight, the crew is energized to save the ship with even more determination. While this scene is imagery, the visual accurately portrays the faith that founders can generate with their belief. Their belief becomes the beacon that is visible for miles. A no-plan-B-for-personal-security founder plunging headlong into the waterfall of chance and coming out on the other end ready for any calamity with a calm mind is the rightful bearer of this beacon.

Building wealth that will be shared with the broader team makes this beacon shine even brighter. Sharing ownership with people contributing to the startup's success is a proactive decision taken right at the beginning and not an afterthought. Try talking to a founder growing a startup for a quick exit designed for his personal gain. They are looking for enough value creation to meet their own wants. Compare his lifeforce to a founder whose goal is to create fifty USD millionaires in his team. There is a night and day difference in the way people respond to this energy.

Being young is great. The body relies on a process called mitophagy to remove old mitochondria. This process slows down as we age and more inflamed cells manage to stay in circulation than before. A startup's metabolism is at its most efficient in its first three years and this is the time for founders to drive the hardest. A founder's boundless energy sets the measure for the startup team to calibrate their own work hours. A founder who puts in fourteen hours at work would get a team to put in at least twelve hours. For ten founding employees, this schedule adds up to 120 work hours a day for the team. A normal team would have put in a regular eight-hour day, failing to realize the additional 50 per cent in productive hours they had the capability to deliver. Not a surprising conclusion then that a startup with 50 per cent more firepower would plough through unanswered questions faster.

Celebrities in their own right, founders get to touch so many hearts with the power vested in them simply with the act of starting up. Starting from the security guard at the entrance, everyone is watching their expressions, moods, tone and body language. The awareness that they can convey so much with how they behave can make them feel like they are giving a performance. Like any performance, this act can give the actor a mild high. Succumbing to these temptations is a slippery slope, where one of the stops is seeking personal brand exposure on media. It is important for the Key to have a chat with co-founders before any large-scale media exposure as it is one of the most unnecessary reasons for founder inter-distancing. Many founders fulfil their school aspirations by becoming suckers for awards and recognition. Before realization sets in, a founder can end up diverting the majority of their energy to outward-driven image management. This fascination with 'the way the world sees me' hampers the energy flow.

A founder has tremendous leverage on energy from all the senior leaders who report to them. First-principle-based business building requires founders to relook at old ways of doing things but once done, their business leaders are expected to adopt and scale the new way. Effective delegation releases founder bandwidth and lets them play to their strengths.

Hiring solid leaders significantly enhances the startup's energy potential.

Regular town halls and daily stand-ups with the team are perfect avenues for formalized energy transmission. A founder's energy need not rely on the spoken word alone to be transmitted successfully. A quick email response, a speedy resolution of a customer issue, or a fast turnaround on a product build—any action done with alacrity can convey this energy.

Celebrating wins collectively as a team transmits energy to the entire team and charges up the atmosphere for more work and collective goal-seek. Wins are more meaningful when they are part of a plan. If everyone joining the celebration can see the achievement as part of a plan and not as an isolated win, it carries more meaning.

A founder who is kind, attentive, optimistic and prone to humour is more likely to make other people feel good about themselves. When people feel good about themselves, they are open to the person who has this effect on them. A founder with the right disposition is able to maximize energy transmission to every member of the team.

As startups age, they face the risk of losing their initial growth trajectory and achieving less and less with each passing year. As the mitochondria becomes less efficient, accumulated waste in inflamed cells is confused for lack of oxygen. It can alternate from energy generation to biosynthesis. The former generates energy while the latter reverses the Krebs cycle to grow cancer cells. When this happens, cells go into fermentation mode by shifting away from their intended function of working to make the whole body thrive to instead aiding the growth of cancerous cells. The life-giving mitochondrion turns into a destructive force.

Faulty metabolism in startups can also cause malignant conditions like a shift to self-preservation versus collective wins. Too many leaders hired from corporate backgrounds too early in the journey can cause this situation. Turfs emerge and department heads emulate corporate-style inter-department rivalry. There is more talk about how another department's inability to deliver is responsible for the loss of traction. Business goals are never adopted by the leaders in their entirety. They carve out the parts of the goal they can deliver and what is outside their purview. The leadership is keen to take over as CEO but not interested enough to make the company win. Their access of control works downwards and headcounts bloat. More headcount represents bigger turf, and so the destruction of value starts.

Sustained stress exposure also damages the ability to metabolize efficiently. A founder may be transmitting large amounts of energy to grow the startup but it may not translate into progress. As startups become larger, their responsiveness to opportunities and challenges declines. Consensus building, meetings and turf ownership block the path of energy flow. Some startups are lethargic even after hundreds of millions of dollars in financing. Some are swift and fast-moving on simple crumbs. Some remain lean and sustain metabolism as they get older. Some glow in self-congratulation after confusing high headcount with success. When this happens, startups slow down and growth begins to crawl.

Certain events sometimes cause the energy of a founder to wither away. These could be a dispute with a co-founder or a product-market fit that remains elusive after years of search. It could be the overwhelming guilt from a declining living standard at home. A competitor's ability to throw sacks of cash at everything could throw off the single-minded pursuit of a capital-efficient founder. A founder who is no longer possessed by the idea of moving forward will get overwhelmed by the hurly-burly of the day-to-day as well as the uncertainty of the 'long road to Ithaca, full of adventure, full of discovery'. When founders get tired or mentally check out, it is immediately visible to the people who work closely with them. Just like a body that is being deprived of energy, a startup with unsteady or declining founder energy is unlikely to thrive or survive. Tired founders will reprioritize and settle for the steady pace with its more predictable outcomes. But a tech startup that tries to find predictability too early in their journey will end up losing talent and capital, which is always drawn to scale outcomes.

Keys are aware that their energy levels have a critical impact on the final outcome. Their approach to working finds all pathways to not only renew their own core of energy but to also transmit as much energy as possible. They remove obstructions of thought, intent and structure to build a startup that is growing and growing fast. They push for growth in the first three years before the additional friction from natural decay sets in. They are aware of their prana and how it is a life-giving force. They know they are not building but growing a startup. They have to cause one cell to multiply into trillions of cells. They have to permeate through all of these cells like 'a cosmic energy [that] shimmers in all stone and steel as well as flesh'.

8

Bouncing Back

'What day is it?'
'It's today,' squeaked Piglet.
'My favourite day,' said Pooh.

—A.A. Milne

All of us fall, get hurt and have bruises to show for it. A founder's falls are numerous. A founder's falls are harder. Founders take calls based solely on their judgement. Some calls fail miserably, but irrespective of what happens, they are required to take even bigger calls. If each situation where a call could go right or wrong were called a tournament, a manager would probably play ten such tournaments in a month. A founder would try and win 100 such tournaments in a month.

An athlete or an individual sports champion has an intense career, which typically lasts five to ten years. If they allow failures in past games to impact their next game, then their careers wouldn't last even two years. Successful athletes have to keep a clean-slate mindset before every tournament.

Michael Jordan, the most successful basketball player of all time, played more than 1000 games in his eighteen-year career. In this period, he attempted 24,537 field goals. Through his long career he managed to stay consistent by winning 50 per cent of his attempts.

Jordan had this to say about his success: 'I've missed more than 9000 shots in my career. I've lost more than 300 games. Twenty-six times I've been trusted to take the game-winning shot—and missed. I've failed over and over and over again in my life, and that is why I succeed.'* Michael Jordan came back match after match after match.

2 April 2011, International Cricket Council (ICC) World Cup, India versus Sri Lanka at Wankhede Stadium, Mumbai. India was chasing a big total and had a faltering start to their innings. Captain M.S. Dhoni was supposed to come in after a very much in-form Yuvraj Singh. He promoted himself up the batting order despite not having a great batting form. On the second ball of the forty-ninth over, Dhoni sent a full delivery from Sri Lankan bowler Kulasekara flying over long-on for a six. India won the match with a bang. India erupted in celebration, and the fireworks went on late into the night. The ESPN commentator had this to say about Dhoni's batting: 'Dhoni had a poor batting record in world cups.

---

* Michael Jordan in an Air Jordan commercial.

Thirty-four was his highest. And what does he do? He promotes himself and played a fine knock to pull this off." Dhoni, who started his international career with a duck against Bangladesh, felt that, 'The pressure had got to me in the previous games. In this game, I wanted to bat up the order and Gary (Gary Kirsten was coach of the Indian cricket team for the 2011 World Cup) backed me. I had a point to prove to myself.'† Dhoni's international career lasted fifteen years.

Like Jordan and Dhoni, Keys are also in it for the long play. This makes it even more rigorous for them because they keep taking on more and more with each successive year, and the years go on longer. And they play at the competitive level of the ICC World Cup, the NCAA, Le Mans, the NBA and the Grand Slams.

What does a founder do when he falls? I am deliberately not using the word 'fail' here because that finality is only an end outcome. The multiple setbacks in the journey are merely falls because the founder finds ways to recover from them. The Japanese proverb *nana korobi, ya oki*—fall seven times, stand up eight—a simple phrase, assumes that the falls will be many and all they require is to keep getting up after every one of them. We can overcome circumstances if we get up just one more time than we fall.

---

* Commentator from Final (D/N), Wankhede, 2 April 2011, ICC Cricket World Cup.
† What MS Dhoni Said After 2011 World Cup Win Sums Up The Leader He Is | Cricket News (ndtv.com).

A founder who stands up after falling for the seventh time will ensure that they stay in the game for the championship title. They will keep a winning attitude and maintain the intensity to push for the big win.

A founder faces two kinds of falls based on the toll they take on their emotional well-being. They have to and will deal with both, but one is less confidence-depleting than the other. One is easier to get over and does not cause a personal sense of failure. The other needs more fortitude to get past.

The first kind of fall happens when some part of the business does not perform as expected. This is not something that needed the founder to take a gut call in determining the course forward. This is an element that is a sub-part in the journey to a destination. Of so many moving parts in a business, some are bound to fail. A screw-up happens. A hire does not work out. A customer is lost. A new geographical market does not pick up. It is painful, but it is business as usual. These issues will keep cropping up. The founder may have a direct role in the fall, but he does not take it as a personal hit. Execution is a collective responsibility with multiple points of falling. Such falls do not weigh heavily on the founder's mind. The damage is temporary. It causes a wastage of time and money but does not put the startup at risk. The fix is straightforward, and the founder quickly goes about setting the situation right.

The second fall results from a strategic choice made by the founder. As founders navigate from one undefined destination to the next, they stop playing safe and seek out non-linear paths. Founders know that there is no road map for this journey because it is uncharted. There will be wrong turns and blind alleys. Falling in big strategic choices like taking a stand on a regulatory constraint, choosing mid-market over enterprise customers, or timing entry into a new market can set the company back by many years and many millions of dollars. The founder is usually the one who takes the final call on such decisions. This type of fall is a harder one to recover from and can potentially lead the company to lose the plot and unravel. A setback of this kind will create a sense of personal failure for the founder. Finding their ship stuck in shallow waters because of poor navigation is something that no captain can shake off easily. The mind is burdened with the risk that the company will face, the loss of face and the self-doubt in taking the next strategic call. When a founder starts to see failure in a fall, it sets a pattern of negative affirmation. A founder's stress response is weighed down with every successive fall. The failure mindset is like quicksand, consuming precious energy in the effort to escape. Over time, this weakened stress response will deplete the founder's zeal and ambition.

I asked many founders about how their emotions typically unfolded after a fall. Most of them said that anger and frustration were the first reactions, which were usually directed outward at the people around them after the first kind of fall. But they burned inward after the second kind of fall.

Founders can catch the self-pity flu in the aftermath of a fall. Sometimes, founders take themselves too seriously, making every fall harder to process. They feel observed by all and sundry. The despair is magnified when they imagine a public viewing of their shameful fall. But thankfully, there is no viewing gallery. Their insecurity is only in their imagination. Founders repeatedly told me that this truth released them from a great deal of unnecessary misery. Investors just want them to make money. Employees want them to succeed so they can have predictability in their lives and also make money. Families understand how hard they work and are the last ones to judge. No one is judging.

Founders would do well to guard themselves against falling into the self-pity trap. Once it sets in, the brain not only questions every choice made but also colours it. The grass on the other side of the startup fence that was not even noticed before now starts looking much greener. A cascade of bleak, unsolvable issues starts to descend across the once bright horizon. 'My investors didn't support me enough', or 'My co-founders didn't carry enough weight.' Their conviction in their own wild plan is shaken. The brain chatters, 'The market is too small. India is not the best place to grow an execution-first business.' Countless reasons to give up start popping up, causing the founder to swerve off course. The founder tells themselves, 'I am putting up a solid fight, but something is not right. I failed. I am not cut out for this.' In this state, founders lose agency and spirit. 'The game I set out to win is not the right one for me.' Finally, the founder shuts down, moves out and becomes a consultant to other startups. If only they had given enough time for their capabilities to compound, their conviction would have strengthened. Instead of questioning the game, they would have gotten better at it. No amount of falling would have pushed them to change course.

As founders mature, they realize that anger is pointless and demonstrating it, even more so. An epitome of composure even during the toughest break points, tennis great Roger Federer did not break a single racquet in frustration through his twenty-four-year career. After surviving many failures, acceptance and analysis become the immediate response to a fall. Self-pity now becomes a dirty word. Founders come to understand that no one really cares about their failure. There is no viewing gallery. Opinions are forgotten quickly. A big weight is lifted off their shoulders. And the response to failure is not as personal and private as before. The fall is handled so much better because now there is no unnecessary suffering. A core feature of a founder is agency. They feel they can control the outcome. The Key tells himself, 'This is the game I want to become the Michael Jordan of, even if it takes me five, ten or fifteen years.' Many founders retire into an isolation chamber to collect their thoughts and then pop back before their teams start to worry. One founder I spoke to shared that every time he fell and needed to bounce back, he would get on to a cricket pitch. At the crease would be a brave batsman ready to face pace bowling. Another founder who I spoke to goes on long walks. Some founders lock themselves in a room with a co-founder, and loud shouting is the only thing that can be heard outside for some time, followed by silence. Some get their teams to chase small wins before the funk sets in, hoping that the small wins recoup the morale drop. The fundamental feasibility of the startup is never in question. The desire is to get better and better at it. The setback is an opportunity to learn more and improve.

In their mind, founders reframe the fall using the locus of control approach that came up in the context of resilient children. Cognitive flexibility allows founders to first accept the situation and then reaffirm their own ability to create a better outcome. Having agency is at the core of the bounce-back process and the founder thrives in it. 'I can get us out of this, I just need to work at it.' That is agency at work.

A founder will go through an inordinate amount of stress. His body will be subjected to the continuous fear of falling. A Key develops a stress response that can sustain them over long wars and short battles. They figure out ways to come out stronger from these long exposures to stress. This response mechanism that they develop is fundamental to sustaining fortitude and physical stamina. To understand this, we need to look at how stress affects our body.

When a stressful situation occurs, the sympathetic nervous system triggers the initial response. Hormones are released, which cause a physical response—the heart rate goes up, muscles tighten. Cortisol is also released when we face stress. Too much cortisol is not good for us. Hence, a neuroendocrine system called HPA axis is responsible for balancing it. The HPA axis not only triggers the cortisol release but also gives feedback to control the amount that is released. A hormone called ACTH released by the anterior pituitary gland binds with receptors in the adrenal cortex to release cortisol.

Cortisol has a wide-ranging impact on our long-term well-being. It affects metabolism and plays a role in the body's anti-inflammatory and immunosuppressive responses. It increases the blood pressure and the sugar level in the bloodstream. The HPA axis is integral to ensure a healthy response to stress. A quick rise followed by a quick drop in cortisol levels is an indicator of a healthy stress response system. When the body has high levels of cortisol over long periods of time, it faces a condition called hypercortisolism. The HPA axis is getting overworked. Founders are susceptive to this condition and go through weight gain, fatty tissue deposits, fragile skin, slow healing of cuts and infections, and acne. The high frequency of stress in these falls can be debilitating unless founders find ways to manage an effective stress response.

George Bonanno is a professor of clinical psychology at Columbia University, New York. He is a leading researcher on human resilience, particularly on response in the context of perception of the event itself. His theory rests on the premise that, as humans, we are all capable of coping with falls.

Bonanno calls this 'ugly coping'.* In ugly coping, we inflate our own sense of self through 'self-enhancing bias'. This ego-boosting trick of the mind is accompanied by repression of negative thoughts and emotions. When shit goes down, we describe it in words to give it context. Some of us hype it up and some of us downplay it. This resiliency theory explores how stress is perceived—the less that is made of it, the less stress it will cause.

Bonanno's study places perception at the core of resilience. How is the fall perceived? Is it a traumatic event or is it an opportunity to learn? According to Bonanno, how we label the fall determines our ability to recover from it. Bonanno would rather have us call it a potentially traumatic event. In this reframing, any negative event has the potential to be seen as a learning event. Bonanno believes that this coping mechanism can be taught. Reframing the emotional response to a negative event in more positive terms will change how we think of the stimuli. People can train themselves to reframe their emotional response, and this training has long-term benefits. Perhaps stoicism was saying this all along when it advocated for maintaining a state of apatheia (not to be confused with apathy), which is characterized by equanimity and freedom from disturbance by external events or extremes of 'passions'. The theory of stoicism emerged in 300 BC in Athens. It

---

* 'The Neuroscience of True Grit', *Scientific American*, 304 (3): 28–33, https://www.scientificamerican.com/article/the-neuroscience-of-true-grit/.

propounded living a well-lived life by following a 'sage' attitude, which entailed developing fortitude and being, well, stoic!

A mega founder will label the fall as a mistake. They will analyse but not overanalyse. In the process, they will move closer to responding like a sage. How a founder mentally labels the fall—as a major setback or as an opportunity to cross another hurdle in the path forward—will determine the ease with which they get back up for the eighth time.

Shunryu Suzuki was a Japanese Soto Zen monk who brought Zen Buddhism to the West. He was appointed to be a teacher of Buddhist learnings at the age of twenty-two. In 1930, he came to the Eihei-ji temple to continue his learning. The temple and its adjoining monastery is one of the largest Soto Zen training facilities in Japan. Set deep in the woods in Fukui Prefecture in Japan, the monastery's zendo seats hundreds of monks who practise non-judgemental awareness or mindfulness. At age fifty-five, Shunryu took over as interim priest at Soko-ji, a Soto Zen temple in San Francisco. *Zen Mind, Beginner's*, a spiritual classic, is a compilation of his talks. The book is considered to be the most influential book on Zen Buddhism teachings outside Japan. The most famous line in this book is, 'In the beginner's mind there are many possibilities, but in the expert's there are few.'*

---

* Philip Kapleau, *The Three Pillars of Zen: Teaching, Practice, and Enlightenment*, (Anchor, 1989).

By practising mindfulness, Zen practitioners maintain the beginner's mind, allowing new insights to emerge. Acting as the opposite of hubris and close-mindedness, a beginner's mind is eager, open and free of preconceived notions. In Zen Buddhism, this state of being in the beginner's mind is called 'shoshin'.

Intellectual humility induces a shoshin mindset and takes effort to develop. But once it is part of the founder's cognitive orientation, every time a fall threatens to chip away at their resilience, shoshin acts as the parachute that will land the mind in the morning after. To develop shoshin, practitioners recognize and observe the small mind, which is chattering continuously about the I-me perspective of any situation. To counter this, the big mind—which is more in the moment and sees the wider perspective—has to be developed by cultivating a broader view of life and nature, which leads to a less dualistic identity.

The practice of shoshin leads to reiteration that new problems are best solved with a fresh approach. Dogmatism is a handicap that limits the ability to problem-solve. Keys get to a state of undisrupted mind in times of failure by adopting shoshin or the beginner's mind. By doing so, Keys are able to traverse new paths without labelling emotions as bad or good. Many Keys whom I speak to are unable to describe their successes or failures in the same way we describe them. There is no emotional baggage weighing down events and achievements. It is just a forward movement.

Founders who operate from first principles bring new eyes to an old problem. Using logic to find new ways to improve the status quo, they figure things out as they go along. There is no preconceived notion of expertise associated with their ability to take the right path. First principle founders tend to be less weighed down by failure because they are aliens in the industries they operate in and rely solely on their ability to take a fresh look at a problem, think without baggage and attempt to solve it. Shoshin is a natural strength especially for founders who execute on the basis of using first principles.

Who do we know in our lives who are the best at bouncing back? They are all around us. Their clothes are red and yellow and green, and they are no higher than two feet. Kids! They are the best at moving forward without hesitation. Something that made them cry a minute ago does not matter any more. They can laugh until they throw up, bawl until they bring the house down, but as soon as the new day starts, they are fully recharged to start all over again. Blessed with infinite curiosity, kids are ready to take on the day with no baggage. They are in the moment, filled with wonder and with no fear of failure. This intense curiosity is driven by the newness of everything—the novelty of eating even a lemon for the first time creates a wondrous experience. This mindset makes childhood a time of immense learning and progress. If we experience events in adulthood in the same way, then our mind will welcome every new thing in our life with open arms. Infinite curiosity in ambiguity is a superpower that arms the Key with a resilient stress-response mechanism. The curious mind is always optimistic. It expects success to be the default outcome, feeds on finding paths through the maze, and remains in a state of forgiveness to self. The curious founder is like the child for whom all missteps are acceptable on the path to experiencing more.

A Key never lets a good crisis go to waste. The momentum vector is always moving forward, and a fall is an opportunity to learn and become better prepared for the next inevitable setback. Every founder I asked about their most certain response to a setback talked about putting in more effort. One founder called it the state of furious action. Furious action is the immersion of mind and body in the building process until it is so all-consuming that no memory of the fall remains. The game is long, and the ambition is to be the best at it. The desire to become the best in the field pushes the founder to be the hardest-working player on the field. A young Michael Jordan, when not picked to play for the team, famously told his college coach, 'I'm going to show you. Nobody will ever work as hard as I work.' Keys often seek to find the performance ceiling in every problem area they are engaged in. They fan out through their network to learn the secrets of the peak performers in the field. There is respect for those who have cracked a problem, and Keys will seek them out to help shorten their learning curve.

Founders need to watch out for not making a classic mistake after a fall. Over time, a founder begins to extend the responsibility of running the startup to more leaders. From tight, centralized leadership, the founder learns to let go and trust others. A structured execution is one in which the team with significant direct responsibility will systematically follow a defined goal-based plan to perform their roles. This style of delegated leadership is most suitable for scaling up the business. It is adopted after the founder has evolved sufficiently as a leader because it requires letting go and broadening the locus of control. A setback challenges the faith in the execution style of others. If the setback raises questions about the structure itself, it can shake the system back to a 'one-person leadership' style. The founder will no longer want the locus of control to be in too many hands. The leaders will be perceived as inept and lacking the founder's degree of self-drive. Leader X is not moving fast enough. Leader Y is not getting their hands dirty enough. The founder will find these faults and pull back control from the leadership team. Future crises and their prevention have no link to the level of delegation but it is the easiest victim. Pulling back from a structured execution delays true scale-up. The remnant feeling after a setback that a founder experiences is instrumental in shaping the future version of the founder.

I have often wondered if there is a link between the widely held Indian belief about the circular nature of time and how Indians approach work. Do Indian founders bounce back differently from their Western counterparts because they believe in this cosmological concept?

If you grew up in India, you were never far from this concept of creation and dissolution. The imagery of Lord Vishnu asleep and waking up is part of the seasons. Vishnu is tired of taking care of Earth and he lets his avatars take over while he catches up on his sleep. These four months are called Chaturmas—a period when the earth becomes wet and dark. The earth uses this period for spiritual cleansing and restarts fresh activity at the end of Chaturmas.

Vishnu goes into a state of slumber at the onset of the monsoon, on the day referred to as Shayani Ekadashi. He sleeps for four straight months around June or July and wakes up only after the end of the monsoon on Prabhodhini Ekadashi. During this period, the earth is considered to be infertile. Humans are expected to dwell on penance. When Vishnu sleeps, the entire world is submerged in flood waters.

After Chaturmas ends around October or November, India goes back to celebrating the fruits of the harvest and a string of festivals follows. Ganesh Chaturthi in September and Durga Puja in October. Hindus celebrate the arrival of the God and the Goddess by worshipping idols. The God come to the home of the devotee and then leaves for the heavens. Their idols, consumed by waterbodies, symbolize the cycle of beginning and end, reminding us that nothing is permanent.

We hear the message of the Gita from childhood: never consider yourself to be the cause of the result of your activities. This involved action but detached result is symbolized by Arjuna's transformation from an unsteady warrior refusing to demolish an army made up of his family to a believer in the notion that the human body and its senses are meant to be discarded as they are just layers of sheath covering the soul.

A quick reflection on the notion of infinite universes from the Bhagwat Purana 6.16.37 can bring about instant humility as it reminds us of our insignificance. Lord Vishnu (or Padmanabha), asleep on the divine serpent Seshanaga, creates the conditions for creation. As he rests on the coils of the timeless serpent swimming in a cosmic ocean, a lotus emerges from Vishnu's navel. Upon this lotus is seated Brahma. As Brahma opens his eyes a universe appears. As Brahma closes his eyes, the world dissolves. Brahma opens his eyes and another universe appears. Brahma closes his eyes and the world dissolves. This continues through the span of Brahma's life of one mahakalpa or 311.04 trillion human years. Then it is said that a new Brahma will emerge from the lotus and open his eyes. And so on and on and on. The vastness of these universes is immeasurable, and this realization of smallness reduces our falls to insignificance.

This humility can propagate the beginner's mind. The concept of the constant cycle of creation and destruction is ingrained in our minds from the stories we grew up with. Those accepting this cyclical view are attuned to the eternal pairing of setback and success.

How the founder emerges after five years of learnings will depend on how objectively the takeaways from the fall were internalized. What worked well and what didn't work? How much blame lies outside the founder and how much needs to be owned? This takeaway validates or refutes the elements of a founder's personal evolution. It can strengthen or shake belief systems. Pulled up by their belief and their curiosity about the unknown, Keys are like the rubber balls whose elasticity lets them bounce right back up with no loss of energy. They conserve their momentum by not paying heed to the imaginary audience and by not thinking of themselves as the all-knowing expert whose fall is an exceptional event. Their resilience is exceptional, and the mindset to achieve it is not an overnight change. As an investor, I would love to find more founders who have this part of their roles figured out well because those who can keep getting up keep getting better, and those who keep getting better keep playing longer, and those who play longest get the big wins.

9

Momentum Makes the
Momentous Happen

'I feel the need, the need for speed.'

—Maverick in *Top Gun*

When observing startups, do you prefer their growth to be like Aesop's tortoise who is slow but steady or the urgency of the White Rabbit from *Alice in Wonderland* who is always 'late, late for a very important date'? Who is the most likely winner in the race to grow a long-lasting company—the wise tortoise or the White Rabbit? The answer may not be that obvious.

Startups that are funded by cash accruals are best off taking the turtle route to success. They have to move at an affordable pace, ignoring the hare who is bouncing along at breakneck speed, not stopping to rest, and risking only those calamities that are manageable with more effort and time, not gobs of cash.

Startups that need external funding before they start generating cash are typically on borrowed time in the form of cash burnt per month of existence. Timeline is equal to cash in the bank. As an investment round closes, the investors wire cash to the company's bank account, and the clock starts ticking. The timer is set to the end of the cash runway. Founders plan an execution roadmap based on the cash available and the milestone that must be crossed for new investors to value the company higher than the last round. The founder knows that if they miss the milestone and the cash runs out, the next round of investors will, in the best case, take them to the cleaners, or, in the worst case, not fund them at all. When there is a price to exist, running like a time-bound White Rabbit is the best choice. The speed at which the startup moves reflects the founder's acumen to use ready playbooks as well as chart new territory to execute and move forward. With the sound of the ticking clock ringing in their ears, the almost paranoid White Rabbit rushes around the wonderland of startups, fearful of missing out on the pole position startups are expected to take if they plan to win the race.

There are other benefits of rushing out through the gate. In an efficient funding world, the biggest outcomes create outsized rewards. A founder who is smart knows that if they have to make the effort worthwhile, they must optimize their time as startup founders. Such founders would prefer to figure out if their startup has legs in as short a time frame as possible. If they feel that their startup will not get anywhere, they would prefer to wrap up and move on to the next venture. This conclusion will allow them to take multiple shots at the prize money. Founders would rather start afresh while they are still young and motivated than plod along, getting old and with no reward in sight. By moving fast, they complete more journeys per unit time, which then allows them to stay on the right side of the age and energy equation. Persistence is great but sometimes the writing is on the wall, and founders and investors refuse to read it. The market has moved on, the outcome won't be large and it's a futile chase to glory but in this realization, a lifetime would be spent. While in practice no founder plans to reach a quick closure decision, but if they do move fast, the early answer is very beneficial in improving the chances of personal success.

What is speed? For one, speed is relative. There is no way to say what is fast or to measure speed in the startup world. The speed that a founder sets as the pace comes with no hard-and-fast rule. Being as fast as possible is considered to be the default speed. When the need to slow down arises, a fast-moving startup can choose to slow down. It is much easier for a startup that knows speed to slow down than for a startup that has only known plodding to speed up.

The great conqueror Alexander was not the best military tactician but he could see the big picture better than any general. Coming from the tiny kingdom of Macedonia, his first action after taking the throne was to announce his plans to take

on Persia, the mightiest empire of that time. He led his army
into modern-day Türkiye to confront the Persian Army under
General Memnon at the River Granicus. The armies faced each
other on the mud banks of the river. Alexander's loyal general
Parmenion advised him to wait until the next morning to
launch the attack. Alexander rejected the conventional practice
of starting in the morning and launched the attack on the same
afternoon. He made sure he was conspicuous by wearing a big
white plume on his helmet and colourful armour. The battle
lasted only an hour. The Persians lost 2000 soldiers against
Macedonia's 120. This battle put Alexander's campaign on
the fast track. Within a year he had defeated Darius III, the
ruler of Persia, in the Battle of Issus in 333 BC. Like Alexander,
Keys make themselves conspicuous by announcing their
growth wins to the public and their goals to a broad audience.
Under the public eye, a startup is unfairly compared to
conventional companies that have been publishing their
half-yearly results for decades. Speed and unconventional
tactics are the weapons available to founders to win against
the incumbents. A startup does not operate at all like the big
elephants they compete with. They travel light and they travel
fast. They can change direction quickly. They can go back to
the drawing board and return to the battle quickly. Speed is
part of their every action and reaction.

Startups that emerge fast and scale quickly are often
criticized for not building a robust enough business model

first. Every time layoffs are announced, every time a startup's culture is called toxic, and every time a startup shuts down after burning through hundreds of millions of dollars, the founder's speed of execution is called out as the culprit. In the event of a high-profile failure, naysayers blame the high-speed train wreck on the recklessness of the founder. Oversimplification results in the root cause analysis pointing to speed being the culprit. The wise reflect, 'The startup moved at breakneck speed, and it was obvious that it would hit a wall and die. They could have taken it slow, been more careful, not squandered their chances.'

And at that slow speed, allow the whole world to pass them by?

I certainly do not agree with this takeaway. I would have a problem if a founder were not moving fast enough. A slow pace should be a choice, not a default speed of execution. For an investor like me, a startup has a finite time to become relevant. There are infinite shots to be taken but in a limited period. The paths that lead nowhere are eliminated by failing fast. This leaves precious time for the paths that show traction and lead to success. Doing more in less time, eliminating, selecting and acting post-haste is the hallmark of a mega founder. Just as in a Pac-Man maze, while avoiding the scary outcomes of being eaten by the ghosts of Blinky, Pinky, Inky and Clyde, Pac-Man races ahead, a founder moves to sweep the space of choices as quickly as he can, no matter the potential scary outcomes. Founders need to answer three vital questions: does the product have utility for someone, is someone willing to pay for it, and are there are many such 'someones'. Speed is a tool that the founder uses to quickly go through various choices to resolve each of these questions.

A startup moves at the rate of answers to these questions obtained per unit of dollars burnt. The founder sets the rate of burning capital based on the type of question. Time is infinite but capital is not. The clock on capital burn is ticking steadily as the race starts. However, finding the answers is not what the race is all about—that is only table stakes. Finding them within the bounds of capital spend, building a profitable business with those answers and setting the pace for competition is the what founders are shooting for. As the rate of questions answered per dollar increases, the startup sweeps the 3D maze of the opportunity at a faster rate. Its competitive edge gets sharper and its lead in the market is established.

The answers add up like the pieces of a jigsaw—each providing a segue for the next set of questions. The first set of questions is preliminary but crucial. The faster the product utility question is answered, the earlier the startup can figure out its ability to charge for it. Quickly answering the pricing question leads to the next question of how many 'someones' will buy the product while the competition is still trying to figure out the utility question. As question sets keep getting answered, the founder can go back to investors with their report card. We found answers to the three vital questions and we did it within the time limit and we did it way faster than anyone else.

F1 pit stop time has reduced from an average of 8.9 seconds in 1990 to 1.7 seconds in 2023. Urgency is not the same as impatience. It is a haste that sets the pace for everyone. It is not driven by the eagerness to win quickly but to play fast. F1 champion Lewis Hamilton captures the essence of speed as he recognizes that as a driver, his 'job is to get into the car and drive as fast and as well as possible'. The goal is speed itself. In an F1 race, the biggest advantage is taking pole position. This position is the prime starting position and the driver gets a straight line to the first corner without the obstruction of cars and turbulent air left by other racers. Lewis Hamilton has taken 103 pole positions in his career, the most in F1 history ahead of Schumacher's sixty-eight. Hamilton ties with Schumacher's seven world titles, indicating a high correlation between pole starts and wins. A startup taking a pole position has a similar advantage of winning the race. It sets the pace for the pack of competitors in its space. Hiring the most talented team members, getting to the sharpest investors in that space, and tying up the most powerful partners and customers are the advantages of staying ahead of the pack. The power of the pole is relevant in both up and down markets. Keys want to move fast and make sure that they take a pole position in the critical steps of company-growing. They drive a sense of urgency that permeates the boardroom and goes out on to the product management floor and the engineering groups.

In their early stages, startups follow a set of playbooks to execute. A playbook is a pre-determined set of choices that have been tried, tested and put together as a recipe to avoid a waste of time. Some playbooks cover how to set up the basic systems needed to be up and running in the shortest possible time while others give the lowdown on how to set up the HR system for a team of fifty or how to start down the search engine optimization (SEO) road. They may not answer the most strategic questions, but playbooks do tackle the steps necessary to set up without an excessive reinvention of the wheel. Some founders prefer to rewrite every playbook irrespective of applicability to their unique situation. Some are unable to apply playbooks because they are constrained by location or budget. Structured playbooks are usually handed down by seed-stage VCs, accelerators and other founders who have been there before. They are an outcome of years of learning. Founders who can access and implement by playbooks can speed up the parts of their startup that are generic.

Just like capital burn, opportunity cost weighs on the speed of execution. Product shipped is better than getting engineering perfected to a T. A founder who thinks too systematically will introduce unnecessary delays by creating processes that cater for every edge case. They will think of building teams for every function and over-hire prematurely. No startup has failed to raise money because their engineering process was bad. In the early stages, the emphasis has to be on product and hype. Hype is about creating a fast-moving jungle fire that needs to enlist opinion-makers before the competition does.

The speed-seeking founders hire teams that are designed to move fast. Mongol armies were known to win battles despite always being outnumbered. Their secret weapon was the speed of their cavalry. The cavalry was broken down into units called 'arban' and each arban had ten men. Every piece of equipment was designed to enable speed of movement. The lightweight Mongol armour was designed to lower the load. An arban could cover an incredible 100 kilometres a day on their sturdy horses. These horses, called Mori, were domesticated 4000 years ago. They stood only 48 to 56 inches to their shoulders and weighed around 500 pounds. Each man had a team of sixteen horses to give them long range. The Mongol Army did not commit its soldiers in a line formation. Small groups would identify weak spots and then a larger force would be committed to charge in. The cavalry used flexible composite bows. These bows needed strength and could be fired accurately from atop the horses because the saddles were designed for stability. Rapid movement was at the heart of every element, including the living quarters, which were flexible and light—a scaled-down version of a sheep wool tent called 'yurt', which could accommodate ten men.

Some of the most notable victories of the Mongol Army, such as the Battle of Mohi against the Hungarian Army or the Battle of Yamen against the Southern Song dynasty of China, saw the Mongols outnumbered four to one. They are known to have won sixty-five major battles and lost only five. A fast-moving startup is similar to the Mongol cavalry. It is designed to move fast and prevent over-committing resources until it is fairly certain which attack point will yield a breakthrough result.

The founder aims to fill the top three or four roles in the product and tech teams with people who have been successful in such roles before. When a founder sets an impossibly huge goal, the time frame to achieve it is driven by the employees' willingness to put in the long hours and weekends. The founder scours the market for the best fit by asking questions from other founders, product folks and engineering heads. They research the profiles of senior employees in similar companies for the best fit for the role. Then they go headhunting. Founders get busy convincing potential hires to quit their jobs and take a fresh bet, as well as determine the right incentive to pay. Of course, eloquently laying out the vision helps in the headhunting tremendously. These hires are most commonly from high-performance teams in other startups. They set a high bar on quality and in turn, hire more people who set the bar high. The pre-knowledge and collective experience of these hires gives exponential speeds of execution and covers up for the time to hire. This contrasts with founders who hire senior leaders through a recruiter. They don't take the time to talk to friends to identify the best possible team. They write a generic brief and hand it to a recruiter and then rely on reading resumes to make a choice. These teams will not set the bar high, and the startup will lack a DNA with bias for action.

In the fast-moving world of startups going from inception to fading away in a mere flash, every quality player is looking for the highest bid to join the right team for the season. Team members tend to get off slow-moving buses because they also have limited career moves to make before they settle down into a small ESOP-big pay cheque senior-vice-president-title job with a less strenuous routine at a unicorn. Everyone is on a clock that maximizes their outcomes. When putting together a startup team, a high opportunity cost for the collective team is the ideal measure of team potential. As ESOP vesting completes, teams coming off from high-speed build phases will begin to look outside for new jobs that offer a fresh slug of ESOPs. Staying on will require the expectation of yet another high phase of growth. Speedy high-growth phases signal valuation jumps to employees who then anticipate valuation multiplication and stick around for the next milestone and further vesting.

Location choices have a significant impact on execution speed. A startup located in a town where it is one of five startups is disadvantaged by the limited availability of execution teams that have playbook knowledge. They are compelled to execute at a pace that the constraints of the location will allow. The founder is now faced with the choice of pushing faster by shifting the startup to a high-pace startup ecosystem or accepting the pace that the culture and team background allows. Startups that are part of a dense cluster of others like them can access people with handy playbooks. They learn from each other, and the knowledge circulates to make new playbooks. Proximity to customers and investors is a major catalyst for the speed of execution. Places such as Silicon Valley, Berlin, Tel Aviv and Bengaluru are centres of major startup activity and thrive on the density of entrepreneurial activity.

A high-speed founder would rather sit in their customer's office cranking out code, taking feedback on their minimum viable product (MVP) daily, and be ready the very next day to take more feedback on the updates. The incorporation of learning is on steroids. The development cycles and time to hack out a feature need to be driven on a sprint to build in all the features for frequent new releases. In contrast, a slower-paced founder will write to customers for feedback, wait a week for them to respond, send them two reminders and receive feedback in the following weeks. As a result, product improvement will stretch over months. The development team will build a culture of long periods between releases.

Startups achieve rapid execution through various methods, one of which is embracing the concept of 'failing fast', which draws inspiration from system design principles. A system identifies failure and stops normal operations instead of running a flawed process. It is applied to lean startups that swiftly move from one tactic to another until the path forward is achieved. This prevents startups from stalling for too long with a possibly flawed tactic.

A startup has a host of inputs like burn on marketing, spending on product development and hires, and throwing new features at consumers. The input is required to drive a certain output rate. Output can be in the form of new paid users added, the churn of users, or simply session lengths. Many startups can control their input side but they cannot manage the relationship between input and output. A founder and his team put in the effort. There is no faulting them for the quantity and pace of work done. They buy ads, ramp marketing, build the top of the funnel and see output at some ratio of the input. They see an uptick in the output, but it is a random quantity. A controlled output would test well when a founder can set a certain goal based on available resources and hit it accurately. When output is required to be controlled, many founders are riding a fast horse, but the horse has a mind of its own. The reins are not in anyone's hands. Pacing fast when the output is a random number is not ideal. Cash burn becomes unpredictable, and it can run out unexpectedly because it is hard to plan a runway. One month the business grows 20 per cent and in the next month, it grows 5 per cent with the same amount spent. To plan the runway, it is imperative to figure out this relationship. Speed-aware founders try and get a handle on the linkage and then work on improving the output-to-input ratio as time progresses. Inward, nose-down periods must follow customer growth phases. This time is spent on answering questions on the input-output ratio. The dollar clock keeps ticking even when the input quantum is reduced. The growth team takes its foot off the pedal and the product team jumps in with their micro enhancements and tweaks to measure the user bounces and drop-off points. The founders set output goals on each traffic light of the user's product journey and the team doubles down to analyse the movement of behaviour on measured doses of input.

Speed in times of crisis takes a different format. When it's time to take an unpleasant decision, most founders will buckle under pressure and let things take their course. They will procrastinate but eventually act, though by then, precious cash, reputation and high achievers have left the premises. Mega founders have a bias for action but they can double it when taking action that involves unpleasantness. The speed they show in cutting through the rot can save startup resources of all kinds. Founders who develop a stomach for unpleasantness can maintain their speed in all situations. Moving fast only in the honeymoon period while slowing to a grinding halt in tough situations is pointless in the quest for pole position. Founders who keep executing at consistent speed cover more ground, answer more questions per dollar and dramatically improve the chance of success.

Sometimes, a lot of activity is confused for speed. Increasing headcount becomes a key performance indicator

(KPI). Action is driven by social media posts. The feeling of satisfaction that arises from watching small groups of well-paid, enthusiastic employees clicking away at their, computers completing a host of meaningless tasks before the weekend partying starts is misplaced. Scaling up at high speed but lacking real direction is a pointless exercise.

In a funding-rich environment, the perverse incentive of setting large goals and running at full speed can happen simply to camouflage the lack of a real spark in the business. The noise around it is a ruse to keep the attention away from the real question, which is related to the plan's viability. Does the idea make sense, and is it meaningful enough?

In such situations, startups that cannot afford to appear lost to the broader world may increase the noise just to make validation appear like a done deal. Of course, they should have more than adequate capital available to burn. Many founders hold on to a business idea only because they remember how hard it was to think it up. Contemplating the effort of figuring out a pivot is exhausting. So, mindless execution continues unabated. That's why conservative VCs want startup funding to be within reasonable limits as excessive funds make it easier to hide under the pretence of speed.

For mega founders, speed is a powerful weapon to drive their startup to success. Like Hamilton's pole record, founders dramatically improve their chance of success by running fast right from the start position. For those odd founders who engage in gaming the system, speed is like the sleight of hand to throw off inquisitive investors from double-clicking on the real progress. Slide after slide about meaningless activity looks impressive to gullible investors who start believing that a lot is going on but in reality, it is a ruse to take up time and pull attention away from the hard questions.

Like the Mongol Army, a startup should be designed for speed. A startup speeds both when it is growing and when it is not growing but is fine-tuning the growth engine. Speed is pointless unless founders have a sense of how to use inputs to create a deterministic output. Speed cannot be a pursuit only during the happy times. It comes to nought if speed is discarded during a crisis.

10

Designing Incentives: Know How to Split the Pie

'Every day is a bank account, and time is our currency.
No one is rich, no one is poor; we've got
twenty-four hours each.'

—Jay-Z

We all love money. It solves most of our problems and when it can't, it still acts as the best measure of our self-worth. A few years ago, a founder I had backed invited me to visit his home in Palo Alto Hills. I drove my rental car up the curvy road, passing golf-course greens and sauntering deer, gaining altitude at every turn until Stanford's iconic clock tower had become a little pin against the blurry backdrop of the bay shimmering in the afternoon sun. At the very top of the hill, I reached my destination—a Spanish-style villa with stone walls and a red clay tile roof. Stretching over a three-acre piece of land, the villa was built in three levels. The founder took me to a spot from where I could see the glass towers of San Francisco.

That's how high we were. It was quiet and the evening breeze got colder with every passing minute. The stillness wrapping every tree and every bush was broken only by the wind chimes. This tranquillity at the top of Silicon Valley became affordable after the founder sold just a fraction of his shareholding in his $2 billion startup.

In every tech city in the world, there is a millionaire's row. Silicon Valley has Atherton and Palo Alto. Beijing has Haidian. Israel has Herzliya Pituah. Bangalore has Kaikondrahalli!

In all these places, fancy houses line the street and founders can be seen pulling out of their driveways in shiny Porsches. Real estate prices rise as startups exit and liquidity flows into the ecosystem.

These are tangible riches that lie at the end of the rainbow. They give incredible purchasing power but despite what they can buy, it is still a tiny fraction of the overall wealth that is created on the making of a successful startup.

The greatest expectation from a startup that raises outside capital is not the kind of house that the founder will live in or the car he will drive. It is the tangible financial value that it will create for its shareholders from its start to its logical end of life. This value is measured in the price that each share will sell at in the private and public markets. The same shares that are worth nothing in the beginning can be sold for millions of dollars in a few years. These shares are tightly held by the founders at the start but get widely held among founders, investors and employees as the years go by. Everyone stands to make a lot of money for taking the risk, which needed adequate incentive to take on, and sticking with the startup for several years.

While there is no hard-and-fast rule, founders would collectively own 5 to 20 per cent by the time there is a major liquidity event like a strategic sale or an IPO. Employees would own around 10 per cent and investors would own the balance. From a $1 billion exit value, founders could become one of the only 2,00,000 people out of the global population of 8 billion to have wealth worth more than $50 million. Employees all together could take home $100 million. Even after taxes, that is a lot of Louis Vuitton bags, Mercedes cars and luxury apartments. The number of LV bags in the closet and cars with stars parked on the porch is linked to the number of shares held by the founders when the startup's valuation jumps to astronomical levels.

Venture investors join in only for the financial upside but key employees join in to take a shot at the glory that comes from working on a belief they resonate with. Some are motivated by the resources and freedom that their role brings. Some compare the compensation they are leaving behind and look for a chance to take a shot at financial security for life. A startup is hardly an easy place to work at. Work-life balance is a joke in a startup. Even those startups that propagate 'play hard work hard' cultures can cause huge stress for the poor employees who do not like to play hard. Startup employees sign up for some amount of daily crap and acidity. They will also run fast and take shortcuts with family time. This delicate balance is not easy to manage in culturally toxic startups despite the attractive monetary benefit. Founders are known to behave obnoxiously, commoditizing humans with the assumption that financial incentive will drive all action. People do not stick around if the softer elements like basic human respect are lacking from a founder.

In most cases of incentive planning, calculating upside works because the methodology to determine the future value is well established. Growth in earnings per share and dividends would determine the future price of a company's share. Two different analysts could independently assess the value, but their estimate would land them in the same range. However, if two analysts try to determine the value of a startup, it could vary by a factor of ten and no one would blink. In June 2014, NYU Stern professor of finance, Aswath Damodaran, well-regarded for his valuation lectures, took a shot at valuing Uber, looking at the business as an urban car service. He valued it at $6 billion whereas private investors had valued it at $17 billion at around the same time. His valuation drew a fair amount of rage for missing the big picture in his conventional model. In 2019, Damodaran flipped his valuation model to valuing the revenue potential from a user and arrived at a value of $58.6 billion. At its IPO offering, the market valued Uber at $82.4 billion. Startup valuations throw off both academia and public markets. The cold objectivity of financial gains works uniquely in startups. Their value remains in the potential/possibility zone even after they achieve business stability and a steady growth. The realization of gain is so uncertain that their value can be derived only as per the 'beauty in the eye of the beholder'.

A founder pitches the future value of their startup. A share in an object of unknown future value is also an unknown number. How would a conversation to determine the incentive quantum proceed with a prospective hire? The founder would say, 'We are certain to hit a $1 billion valuation in five years, so your 1 per cent should net about $10 million.' And the prospective hire would likely respond, 'When I look around, the odds of anyone hitting $1 billion in valuation are so low that I think at best you may hit $500 million—and it's more certain that you will reach around $250 million. And 1 per cent in such an outcome would be about the same as what I would make collecting a pay cheque in my current big company secure job with its annual bonuses.'

A startup's chances of success are hard to fathom. The quantum of incentive varies by everyone's aspirations but it is dependent on the environment and their take on the chance of success. How then do founders offer incentive-sharing in a mystery box, where a consensus on its future value would require both sides to take a leap of faith?

For an employee, perceiving lower risk is a big driver to sign up to a financial incentive of unknown proportion. Age has a lot to do with risk-taking. Freedom from monetary party poopers like home EMIs, children's education costs and supporting the family is usually the domain of the young and restless. No wonder then that the dominant population of a startup census is below thirty years.

An overfunded venture market plays tag with an optimistic environment. Rising valuations, early exits and a seemingly never-ending supply of cheap money perpetuates over-optimism. And on the reverse swing, the opposite of these factors causes excessive pessimism.

In overfunded environments, startups are flush with funds. For professional leadership that is being hired from large corporations, salaries need to be made at par with their stable job salary. Hires are made on the basis of 'hey, I can't afford (of course you can!) a drop in my take-home pay cheque, but the promise of the upside from the equity portion is very compelling'. Many corporate career backgrounders come seeking the unstructured excitement of a startup life but don't want to compromise on their take-home salaries. This misplaced sense of risk is prevalent in markets where the ESOP culture has not yet started consistently delivering on its promise. As founders talk incentives to corporate employees with eight-figure salaries, they run into the challenge of 'already achieved most adult-life material goals'. The motivation to earn more than this may be thin, so where does an incentive conversation start? If people behaved rationally, they would stick to their fat salaries and reasonable balance of home and work. The risky nature of the startup would be a serious deterrent. When funding becomes tight and startups can't afford $500,000 salaries, they don't hire professional business leaders. Instead they lean on professional risk-takers—ex-founders who have built their financial safety net already or have an appetite for risk with widely varying outcome possibilities.

The prospect theory, proposed by Israeli psychologists Daniel Kahneman and Amos Tversky, forms the basis of all of behavioural economics. Their collaboration between 1971 and 1979 won Kahneman the Nobel Prize in Economics in 2002 (Amos passed away in 1996 and the Nobel Prize is not awarded posthumously). Their theory was centred on the claim that most people do not behave in a perfectly rational way. If we try to understand risk-taking behaviour in incentivization at startups by using the prospect theory we start from the numerous biases in intuition. People reference the decision to their personal situation, so a gain or loss has different value in different incentive conversations. In periods when they see their more enterprising friends sitting on employee shares notionally worth millions of dollars, they feel a sense of loss, and this lowers their sense of risk for the success potential of startups in general. During such periods, they will value the reward outcome to be on the higher end of the band—if the founder positions the end value at $1 billion, they would discount it to $750 million. When employees evaluate startup options in down markets, their perceived risk is far higher than rational. If the founder positions the end value at $1 billion, they would discount it to $100 million. In down markets, holders of large portions of option shares are known to move out in droves. Working in a high-risk startup as a way to solve for a mid-life crisis no longer seems attractive. The fancy car in the driveway is a far more attractive way to achieve the same goal.

The prospect theory also suggests that the 'awesomeness' of financial rewards flattens out beyond a point. Getting more money after that point fails to create marginal attractiveness. Do founders remember the need to play on the rationality gap in decision-making when they discuss incentives with their hires? Do they understand that the perceived value of the amount of equity being offered to individual leaders could vary based on the individual's flattening point? In my limited survey, a generic approach is followed, and incentives are more or less designed with a cookie-cutter approach. It relies on the ubiquitous hunger that is latent in every mind in a growing economy. This craving is a boon for the startup ecosystem and for the founders who need outcome-driven employees.

What we know from talking to startup employees from ventures that have been practising incentive design over a longer period of time is that an individual's reference frame to having enough wealth is the doing away of the dependence of working for someone for the rest of their lives. The expectation flatness point breaks out at the level of what Urban Dictionary defines as 'f-you money'. The definition describes it as 'any amount of money allowing infinite perpetuation of wealth necessary to maintain a desired lifestyle without needing employment or assistance from anyone'.* The first spend from a large payoff is usually a home followed by stylish wheels until the leftover is handed over to a wealth manager to grow. Surprisingly, a large part also goes back into the ecosystem in the form of seed cheques. This is considered most gratifying as it is seen as a sort of give-back to the ecosystem. The acquisition of this kind of capital can free the mind from the decades of conditioning to first check the right side of the menu. A couple of million dollars in one go gives most people the opportunity to live life on their own terms.

If we think of the incentive pool as one big pizza to start with, then throughout the startup's journey, the founder has a knife in their hands and carves up this slowly disappearing pizza. They start with the whole pizza and then, as people keep joining the startup, they cut a slice and hand it over. Investors take more slices in exchange for a cash investment. What is left over in the end is for the founder to keep. The more they give, the more

---

* Urban Dictionary, https://www.urbandictionary.com/define.php? term=fuck +you+money.

hands and capital gather around the table to build the business. The more they give, the less they have left for themselves. If the startup is capital efficient, it would require fewer slices to be split and given away. This would leave a bigger size of slice in everyone's hand, including the investor and the founder. Everyone benefits. But conversely if the startup is expected to be very valuable, it would take many more slices to be shared. There will be less left over in the end for the founder but if more splitting was a good decision, then the value of the startup will indeed make up for the smaller piece left over.

The first cut happens at the starting point when the founders decide to split the pizza among themselves. Ownership in the startup is an incentive that founders need to commit extraordinary energy day after day for the foreseeable future. Like many founders say, money is not important until it is. And once it is, it also serves as a quantitative measure of success. No wonder unicorn status remains an aspirational club.

Founders are bright people and have a higher-than-average opportunity cost. They are pooling in their resourcefulness and fortunes for a joint outcome. There is massive interdependency and a combination of trust, feel-good and belief at work. These factors are far more important than the discussion on splitting the equity. Some founders are instinctively so comfortable with each other that the instant they shake hands, they are in sync on the split they are most comfortable about. These founders probably know each other from the past, perhaps even from college, and can't imagine growing the startup with anyone else.

The not-so-lucky ones don't get to a happy number that easily. They are not yet sure of each other's commitment or strengths. Usually, the conversation's awkwardness pushes it out to a point where it only becomes more awkward. The obvious solution of finalizing the split of ownership this early in the process is hampered by issues such as hesitancy and uncertainty. Keeping it simple always works best.

Founders are better off splitting equity equally when they know each other and have worked together long enough to know the unique strengths of each individual. To the outside world, equal splits reflect higher collective strength coming to the table. Strength that each of the co-founders is accepted as an equal. Keys could choose to split the equity equally without compromising on how they feel about their outsized commitment to stay forever and own the bulk of the build effort. This would set the mark on how they feel about the value that their co-founders bring to the table. For VCs, it's good to hear what each founder sees as value coming from their co-founders and linking it to how they decide to make the first cut of the pizza. Equal splits are good because they are simple and leave no room for dispute. On the other hand, unequal splits that are not too lopsided and have been arrived at after much deliberation on individual strengths are thoughtful. They are closer to optimum incentivization for each founder. The inter se distribution of equity among founders is an indicator of the relative value that they bring to the table. A Key holding 50 to 60 per cent of the pizza and leaving the rest for one or two co-founders with ownerships of at least 20 to 25 per cent is still considered well-balanced.

Lopsided splits where one founder owns more than 80 per cent and the balance is split among the others with co-founder titles are an indication that the team is not really a multi-founder team. The gap is so huge that it raises questions about the qualifications of the co-founders. Also, is a 10 per cent starting ownership enough of an incentive for the co-founder to continue building at the same pace as someone who owns the lion's share?

I have come across countless instances of co-founders departing their startups prematurely because a simmering emotional tension around leadership boils over. Equity split has nothing to do with it. It could have been equal ownership between two founders and yet a lack of acceptance of the Key's role leads to an unfortunate separation. An uneven split early on is sometimes helpful in figuring out that there is a Key in the startup who will lead it forward and will step in to save it, without needing consensus in both cases.

The pressure on founder equity builds up when the investor rounds cause dilution. Sometimes pivots and expensive rounds cause the founder's equity to reduce by as much as 70 per cent. Founder incentives are severely compromised, and this imbalance needs to be fixed by adding back some equity to the founder pool from the investor pool. This is whacky in traditional incentive-linked behaviour terms because, as the drivers of the business, the founders were 100 per cent responsible for causing their ownership to suffer from heavy dilution. Now the same set of people are asking for and, in most cases, being given additional equity to continue their onward journey in peace. Failure is being subsidized by the investors because the founders need incentives to continue building. Does this create a fallback option for founders that their equity is insured beyond the normal level of dilution? This depends on the belief the investors have in the founders' ability to create value. While most investors do not have the foresight to appreciate this, top-ups ensure that founders do not turn into parasites with agency. The mindset of 'I don't own anything meaningful but everyone lets me behave like a founder with a free run' can lead to reckless brinkmanship. Their downside is now so low that they would rather create value in a new venture where they own a lot more. They start spending more time in the new venture while pretending to run the old one. The new venture mooches the best people and capital off the old one and the unfortunate investors continue to believe that all is well.

Incentives are often turned on their head in the venture world.

The right incentives for the right people have been employed in the pursuit of big-win-low-probability-of-success expeditions over the ages. The formula is the same. Identify the Key. Spell out the reward. In the event of success, make sure that the reward is fructified.

Whaling was an attractive high-stakes venture. It could create big wins for capital and crew. But a successful whaling expedition was rare—two-thirds were unprofitable and a high percentage never came back to shore. A successful trip would fetch $150,000 on a risk capital of $25,000. The captain would get to keep 10 per cent of the earnings and a first mate would make 5 per cent. The share of the remaining earnings would trickle down to the entire crew who put their lives at risk in a high-odds outcome. Despite the dangers of capsizing, and loss of lives and capital, the rewards ensured a continuous flow of daring crew who preferred fat rewards with high risk rather than a trickle of small compensations.

The Mongol Army, perhaps the most successful organization in warfare, also relied on incentive design for success. Genghis Khan replaced the seniority system by elevating commanders based on merit. Every commander was motivated to succeed because they knew that there would be an equal distribution of the winnings. The ESOP equivalent system was called 'jarqu', which ensured that the distribution was administered correctly. Winnings in the form of precious metals, land and tributes would flow to commanders. They would ensure that conscripted men were paid a fixed salary and some share of the winnings.

A cleaner version of this cooperative structure came into being in the mid-1950s on the US West Coast. The owners of the San Francisco-based newspaper *Peninsula* were keen to keep news in the hands of the employees when they retired. Tax laws and cost of transfer hindered the handoff. The owners hired a forty-two-year-old lawyer called Louis Kelso. Louis believed that American capitalism was at risk due to the increasing concentration of wealth, and the solution to this problem lay in finding a way that would allow 80 million American workers to own stock and earn dividends. Louis devised a unique way for *Peninsula*'s employees to buy the newspaper with a loan that repaid itself from the newspaper's earnings. He got the tax authorities to allow this form of borrowing and coined the term employee stock ownership plan, or ESOP.

Soon after, in 1957, Arthur Rock helped the 'traitorous eight' form Fairchild Semiconductor. Eight disgruntled employees of Shockley Semiconductors, tired of the paranoid management style of their Nobel-awardee boss William Shockley, sought to branch out on their own. As their banker, Arthur Rock not only arranged financing but also put together a cap table that allotted 100 shares to each of the 'traitorous eight' and reserved 300 for future employees.

ESOPs convert the spirit of 'it's your company so we share the value creation' into precise financial maths. As the value of the company grows, the value of the share increases. Individual contribution can pool into the collective win. Everyone is aligned to make the company win and individual differences are relegated to the background.

The size of grant of options to early employees depends on the generosity or desperation of the founders. Most founders I spoke to about using a framework to determine the quantum to early employees had no answer. As long as the numbers were reasonably small and the headroom of available options was large, these grants were easy to negotiate because the early employees were those whose belief in the founders was more or less blind. Despite being the largest risk-takers, this lot takes a big dose of the unknown and settles in, often unfairly, on a promise that is never fulfilled. Some founders have this conversation in two parts. In the first part, founding employees come and work for six months to test the waters and estimate their value add, and in the second part, they return to the negotiating table to discuss the quantum.

As the startup grows into a corporate, incentive becomes more structured, and it becomes easier to use market benchmarks to pick a number to start the negotiations with. The head of sales is getting x per cent in a Series D, and a CTO is getting y per cent in a Series E company—these data points are available to provide a reference point. Similarly, salary data is available in the market by position and stage of company.

Mega founders are ready to cast aside these benchmarks. They do not nickel and dime when it comes to sharing meaningful equity with top contributors. Judging value lift is the critical factor in the decision. What is the primary driver that adds or protects value from hereon for the next three years? And who can deliver this? Once the need is mapped to the resource, incentives are at work to tie it all together.

Founders take a case-by-case view on the top contributors who can steepen the trajectory of the startup. They are willing to eat into the pool for the right team member. Their judgement comes into play when they decide how much they want to lean backwards and for whom.

A seasoned CTO helped push an overly execution-focused startup to a product-led business model. A US sales leader helped a startup break into the North America market, triggering a global venture capital firm to invest. A head of product released a founder's bandwidth so he could focus on monetization. I have seen these hires add hundreds of millions of dollars in value to startups by solving critical inflection problems. All three situations were value-creating, and the incentives were clearly established because the value seek was spelt out and set as bearings.

What is the life expectancy of the incentive? While adding some more shares to renew the faith in the relationship is always a possibility, the lion's share of the incentive is the first chunk. For all recipients of shares except investors, the clock starts ticking on receipt and ownership strikes equally over four to five years. This ensures a balance between the creation of value and the reward handover. The incentive is tightly linked to outcome and the time spent.

The price run-up on the shares is entirely market-driven— it can take forever or happen overnight. Founders worry about making their employees fat and happy too early on in the journey fearing they will not care to work any more. Investors worry about their founders selling their equity in private sales before the investors cash out. The question to ask at this point is whether the realization of some value is likely to slake the appetite or whet it further. Late investors routinely allow founders to cash out tens of millions of dollars of stock. The reason? They believe that the founder can only give billion-dollar outcomes if they have seen and experienced the fruits of a hundred-million-dollar outcome. If they have bought the villa and the Mercedes and the Guccis and then another villa in Dubai, they will eventually need the private jet. For that to happen, they will have to reset their material need clock to the XXXL-sized outcome.

When startups create liquidity for ESOPs by establishing regular programmes for employees to sell their shares, they create a healthy sanctity of their value. Employees believe in potential value and the trust keeps building. Founders who make sure that new investment rounds allow for liquidity for their employees are creating a very strong reinforcement loop. They are satisfying the aspirations of hundreds of employees. A mass wealth creation process has a multiplier effect on the ecosystem, and its reverberations are felt far and wide.

Real estate prices in Silicon Valley rise in areas where employees of a startup that recently had an IPO buy their new homes. Bankers swarm these neighbourhoods for signing up new asset pools.

My visit to the founder's mansion in Palo Alto Hills was wrapping up. The trip rekindled my belief in the power of the right incentives. The hill on which we stood as we watched San Francisco's skyline 50 km away rested above the valley where many other employees of successful technology startups had bought their multimillion dollar homes from the proceeds of their stock options.

Mega founders slice their pizza with a lot of thought. They create trust-building mechanisms so that incentives are seen as sacrosanct promises. They value scarcity and yet give generously when they can tie value builders to delivering critical outcomes needed to cross each growth inflection. Incentives build startups. Incentives compensate for lost time. They heal bodies and minds.

11

Head on Shoulders

'Man, it's so hard not to act reckless
To whom much is given much is tested
Get arrested, guess until he get the message
I feel the pressure, under more scrutiny
And what I do? Act more stupidly
Bought more jewellery, more Louis V
My mama couldn't get through to me'

—'Can't Tell Me Nothing', Kanye West

Suburban Superkid revved his BMW on the one road in the city that had no potholes—the highway to the airport. The car responded with a controlled purr to every tap of the accelerator. The machine was designed to satisfy a man's urge for controlled exhilaration with zero emotional expectation. Superkid's startup had just closed its Series D round and now the company's bank account of $55 million gave it the largest war chest of free-to-burn cash in the space. He had worked hard for this round and with late-stage investors becoming increasingly rare, it had been touch and go. The TwinPower Turbo V8 engine pushed the car forward with an incredible 617 horsepower packed under its hood. Superkid let himself bask in this moment of triumph. He felt the same happiness that he had felt when he saw the proud look on his parents' faces after winning the Best All-Rounder trophy at seventeen. He was already easing up on the throttle as the toll barrier approached when the biker came from nowhere. It was the black helmet that hit the windscreen first. The crash was deafening.

The party had not stopped for Natkhat National. His life had been a blur ever since his startup had closed its Series A round of $10 million. He had been picked for a '30 under 30' award and thanks to his way with social media, his life was now being showcased by the media. Party invites were never-ending, and his stamina made him the life of every party. Relationships had never been his forte, but thankfully, with his startup on a roll, he had no time for a serious commitment. On the morning of the last weekend of March, his CFO was charged with siphoning money out of the company's account. Business came to a standstill. An inquiry by the board was expected to throw light on the reasons, but Natkhat knew that it would be hard to survive this body blow. The party had stopped.

Smalltown Studious' wife had just walked out on him, taking their three-year-old daughter with her. He had tried to understand why she was constantly grumbling but could only explain it as the stress from managing a home and taking care of a toddler. He simply couldn't figure out why she called him emotionally stunted. She would complain about his aloofness and inability to communicate. Sitting alone in the empty house, mindlessly playing with his daughter's plastic pony, Smalltown just couldn't match his view of his persona to this alien that his wife had painted him to be. He connected with everyone and could talk to his team for hours. The years had been tough, but he had worked so hard for all of them. The night seemed long as he uncorked the new bottle of Scotch to contemplate his life.

These are moments when worlds come apart without warning. We are flying at the top of the world, looking at the future with a warm feeling in our stomach. Our lives look perfect until, out of nowhere, a big bolt of lightning comes crashing down to remind us that the screen of solidity has been hanging by a thread that we did not see. We are blinded by the control we are able to exercise on our little kingdoms until life teaches us that a body blow could come from the most unexpected place. The act of remaining grounded does not deter this big bolt of lightning but it gives us a protective shield. Not soaring in the air current of success is a tough ask.

Remaining grounded is not an exercise in range-bounding our emotional swing. Most of us stress about our goals, achieve a little, pat ourselves on the back and then don't revisit the stress for months. Sometime we fail and stay in a state of paralysis for as long as it takes to nurse our shaken confidence back to normal. We read the Gita and often wonder what is meant by the instruction to 'remain indifferent' to outcomes. We try to act dispassionately to reduce the pain of failure. The pendulum swings are meant to get smaller on the sides of both sadness and happiness but more often than not, it is the happy side that reduces while the sadness side gets larger. The goal to find equanimity remains elusive. In such a life of range-bound emotions, we are shying away from strong feelings. Remaining grounded is relevant only when we let ourselves go deep into feeling the sharp pain of failure and the wild exhilaration of success.

Founders are on a cramped schedule of emotional upheavals. They are either winning or losing. Never still. They 'do' so much in so little time. They knock off goal after goal. They ride a roller coaster of emotions. High and low. Low and high. Founders are no passive monks solemnly observing their lives play like a movie on a screen. They are in the movie, playing out their roles with gusto, deeply breathing in every emotion that the scene demands. One moment they are flying in elation and in the next moment, they are drowning in sorrow. All physiological parameters in the brain, gut and heart exhibit a visceral connection to the emotions playing out.

Founders behave like military generals. They are the Napoleons and Alexanders of our times. Permanently placed in charge. Pushing people to do their bidding. Ordering them to jump over fire pits and climb steep fortress walls. Having people blindly jump into a pitched battle creates an acute sense of responsibility, but it also intoxicates. Napoleon, normally a brilliant military strategist, made blunders as he had been lulled into a state of complacency by a long winning streak. Founders have driven their perfectly sound businesses into the ground in similar states of arrogance and invincibility. An intoxicated founder will give directions to his troops with consequences that echo famous historic military disasters: marching an army across snow-covered country with little protection against the cold; ordering the troops to drag heavy guns across rain-soaked ground, resulting in their wheels becoming mired in the mud. Many soldiers have died solely because their general's judgement was clouded by hubris. Objectivity becomes muddled because the brain has been fed a diet of testosterone.

Founders are at great risk of not being able to remain grounded because they are wired to remain buoyant, downplay falls and remain wildly optimistic. As they become successful, they are beset by a phenomenon in biology called the Winner Effect. Thanks to its magic, a gorilla who has won fights against weaker opponents is likely to overcome a stronger opponent. According to neuroscientist Ian H. Robertson, this works for humans too.[*] Humans who have won in the smaller battles are more likely to win the big battles too, compared to an incumbent or someone who starts off with a loss. The theory suggests that success rewires our brain, making us more

---

[*] Ian H. Robertson, *The Winner Effect: The Neuroscience of Success and Failure*, (Thomas Dunne Books, 2012).

focused, confident and aggressive. Ian H. Robertson comes from the Nietzsche school, which gives hope to humans as agents and not 'subjects of their emotional stress'. The hardware of the brain is co-dependent on the software of the mind. The chemicals are not secreted in isolation. The software has a role to play in how the hardware operates, and humans have a say in how the software should work. Trader-turned-neuroscientist John Coates in his book *The Hour between Dog and Wolf: Risk-Taking, Gut Feelings and the Biology of Boom and Bust* explores the role of a feedback loop that winning creates by improving the chance of winning the next game. Biologists have studied animals closely for this behaviour. They observed that after removing all biases, animals across species who win a fight for turf are likely to win the next fight as well. Coates compares this behaviour to humans on the sports field and to humans in the trading ring. In a tennis match, the winner of the first set goes into the second set with heightened testosterone, which greatly improves their chances of winning again.

A founder goes through the biological feedback loop caused by the Winner Effect. Testosterone and dopamine are released when the founder's brain experiences a win—shipping the product on time, crossing 10,000 users, signing a big partnership, making an important hire. The founder is that one person who is at the heart of every win. A founder's centrality to the startup's success—big or small—makes them susceptible to the on-the-loop secretions of these feel-good hormones, often turning them into a monster with an invincibility complex.

Dopamine's relentless 'need a high' loop rewires the brain. Failures feel so deep and dark that the high is guzzled by the brain with abnormal gusto. The swing in the brain is so extreme and frequent that that delusion becomes a part and parcel of existence. Founders live under conditions that cause them to separate from the normality of human existence. Delusion-causing events are many in a founder's day. Always a David in a Goliath's world, the founder lives in a world that expects them to perpetually seek victory with a slingshot. It is an unforgiving existence, where failure is not an option.

People around founders start to treat them like superhumans, bestowed with the ability to think up solutions on the fly and execute them like no one else. In the early days of the startup, a founder solves problems of all kinds, from the mundane to the complex. As the startup grows, the thorniest problems still bubble up to the founder. Founders know that while their plate of problems is always painfully full, their abilities are unique and surpass everyone else's. Even the most expensive professional hire with a superlative resume pales in comparison to the founder's deadly combination of creativity and execution ability. This perpetual dependence on founders puts them in a 'saviour' mode. The saviour mode can inflate the ego like a balloon. An ego that seeks to be fed with adulation will attract many courtiers willing to fawn over their god. Hidden amongst the normal junta, sweetening their dispositions with honey-coated tongues, they pander to the ear's hunger for praise. Fondling and caressing the god's growing identity, they create a temple inside the organization and install the founder's statue in its sanctum sanctorum, acting as priests carrying symbols of delegated authority over the other employees.

With every successful milestone, the chance of a founder losing his head increases. Founders are required to commit to a path full of risk at every turn—failure dampens the spirit but success seduces. Founders can feed off this and tune out subsequent risk from their mind. A startup run by a founder whose sense of business risk has become warped by personal invincibility is committed to eventual doom. Ravana, Mahishasura and Viradha in Hindu mythology exemplify this arrogant state of mind that ended in their destruction.

The freedom that a founder gets to run his startup gives him a free hand to bet the farm if he wants. For the long-term success of the startup, it is absolutely necessary that the founder keeps their head on their shoulders. If they cannot do it, they should step away.

All mega founders I spoke to about the risk of losing their minds use the 'day one' reminder. When they find themselves feeling distracted with early success, they remind themselves of the size of their vision. That vision in which the size and scope of the business is a distant speck on the horizon. The present state is just a milestone in a long journey. A reminder that the mountain peak is yet to be climbed is instantly grounding. It can reset the smugness and complacency that comes with early success. This effective reminder is powerful in its simplicity. Remembering that the place they need to reach will take a lot of effort creates the sense of a new journey. It puts into perspective the magnitude of past success against the effort to achieve the final goal.

A founder who can avoid being seduced by their own achievement will ensure that their dream lives beyond them. A founder can prevent their succumbing to this ever-present temptation by letting go of absolute unchecked authority. They make themselves answerable to a board that represents the broader interest. The pressure to justify their actions makes them accountable. It requires them to be transparent and seek approval before committing to major decisions. A strong board will keep the founder's ego in check. A strong board will ask uncomfortable questions and force thoughtful action.

Some founders justify bad behaviour as a revolt response to one too many voices of caution. 'My board is filled with idiots. They don't understand my vision. Caution doesn't win wars. I am fighting the war, and I know how to win it.' The mechanism that is put in place to rein in unchecked authority is made out to be the adversary. A mega founder crafts his board with care, balancing cautionary voices with those who have been in battle before. He pays heed to both. Caution is not an inhibitor—it does not evoke groans and visions of chains. It creates the picture of guard rails along the path.

A Key should be backed by a posse of capable leaders with enough trust cache when the company's failure can only be brought about by a faltering founder. That posse of leaders could be the original members of the founding team or laterally hired professionals. The handing-over matters more than to whom the handover is done. The idea is that a founder should be comfortable letting go of their control over everything to this battery of people. With a multi-leader operation, not only does scale-up become possible but it also reduces the head-swelling that the single point of dependence causes for the founder. The founder needs to learn how to manage multiple leaders. This will force them to be dispassionate and shift their focus to managing people from managing problems. This transition is itself a maturity progression that all recognized business leaders in the industry have mastered at some point in their lives. Industry leaders in traditional sectors like banking and healthcare have shifted their engagement style from the I-will-save-the-day Iron Man approach to the make-sure-everyone-remains-calm Nick Fury approach. Nick's Winner Effect is spread over so many heroes that Nick can remain collected and present in every situation. This transition is what separates so many promising startups that will never become publicly listed profit-making companies from the heavyweight stocks traded on a public exchange.

Media overexposure is not a recommended antidote to a swollen head. India is a land of millions of gods and demons. Hero-worshipping is a national timepass. With social media supercharging this practice, the popularity ascent is quickly followed by a descent. Any founder unfortunate enough to become a social media favourite is in for a nasty surprise when the attention shifts to someone new. Founders need to see the pointlessness of image management. The media stories are just spaces being filled for consumption and clicking. The best place to build is away from the public, but sometimes the spotlight helps. Mega founders know when to withdraw from public attention and when to use it to achieve their goals.

There is a strong component of luck in a startup's success. A founder on a winner's high will discount the role of luck. 'It was all me. I made the right choice.' Those founders who want to stay grounded will credit luck to a greater degree while those who are taking the train to Arrogance City will attribute success to their own brilliance.

I have seen mega founders indulge in luxury symbols yet continue to exert power over material objects rather than the other way around. The world behaves differently with a person who wears a glittering proclamation of 'we are rich' on their body. The fawning treatment that the service industry bestows on the bearer of these symbols is a new feeling. It pulls the person out from the massive well of a billion undifferentiated humans making the same fashion statement in their affordable mass wardrobes. This feeling can lead to the subconscious conclusion that everyone is smiling for the person and not for the symbols. Mega founders are able to get over this feeling and move past their indulgences. They do not become victims of the machinations of the luxury fashion industry. Early wealth affects the founder's home in different ways. A spouse may not be interested in flaunting the ultra-luxury label on their clothes and shoes. Or a spouse may be more interested in displaying some spoils of war in their peer group.

A founder spends his entire day in the bowels of his kingdom. Holding absolute authority, he carries an aura of power. He walks the corridors with regal grace, deliberate and confident. No matter how much time a founder spends at work, he has to go home and sleep. When he goes home carrying the authoritative persona with him, he misses an opportunity to get his ego recalibrated. Just as he has co-founders at work, he has a co-founder at home for the bigger purpose of life. His home is meant to be a retreat, a sanctuary where the mind gets to disengage. It evokes warmth in the heart and an automatic unclenching in the muscles. Threats reduce and stress dissipates. But not all homes generate this reaction. Smalltown Studious could not fathom why he felt miserable coming home. He felt unhappy, perplexed as to why his stratospheric self-worth in the outside world would plummet as soon as he entered his own home. He should have the same fawning courtiers at home.

Fragrant plumes from the sandalwood incense sticks placed at the foot of his golden statue should envelop his house too. The air should vibrate with hymns about his widely acknowledged indispensability and omnipotence. But instead, the complaints don't stop. At home he is just an emotionally awkward, uncommunicative person who is perpetually missing from the business of living life.

Smalltown Studious is the 'hamara beta' who is doing so well in life. His parents will be proud of him. His ambition stands as testimony to the successful job of raising him. Like his parents, most parents choose not to stand in the way of their children's ambition. The glory will roll up whenever he is successful and that will be enough. But the beta is also someone's husband and father. When he goes on a mission to build a startup, he will be physically and mentally checked out on the home front. His wife and children will live their lives as if he does not exist. His wife will suffer the emptiness of a partner who is in absentia, an incomplete home and singlehandedly deal with the stress of raising a family. Just because her husband is building a unicorn, her life will not be filled with a sense of accomplishment. She will experience emptiness where the founder will experience fulfilment. She will need her own life to become meaningful before she can become a happy partner to Smalltown. Until then, the circle of stress will continue not only for her but also for Smalltown. They will grow apart.

Their lives will not intertwine and the balm that a home should provide will become another source of stress. The founder will not find any window to turn off his constant spikes of cortisol.

Unfair as it sounds on their time, a founder is better off making up for their absence from home with an explicit effort rather than hoping that a relationship defined by society will accept his success as a replacement for his long absence. Founders need to see their personas, their homes and their startups like the three balls in a juggling act. This switch is hard because internal wiring is not easy to change, but we are talking about the act of balancing life for as long as possible. Juggling is at least as old as its earliest depiction on the wall of a 4000-year-old Egyptian tomb. Jugglers catch clubs, rings and balls to create a mesmerizing image that looks impossibly fluid. The father of information theory, Claude Shannon, was a mathematician, electrical engineer, computer scientist, cryptographer and amateur juggler. He represented the most basic juggling pattern, the three-ball cascade, through an equation. The theorem equates one complete cycle of the juggle measured in time that the ball is in the air and the time that the ball spends in the hands. According to the equation, the number of balls that can be juggled is dependent on how quickly the hand can switch from being empty to full and how high the ball must be thrown to give the hands enough time to move. The theorem sets a limit for the number of balls that can be juggled, because as the balls increase, the margin of error in tossing speed reduces. The rate of juggling is measured by the dwell ratio. Dwell ratio is represented as the fraction of time that a hand holds a ball to the time it spends in the air. If the dwell ratio is small, the number of balls in the air is large, giving time to the juggler to modulate. Anthony Gatto, one of the best jugglers in the world, holds a number of records, one of which is keeping nine balls in the air for fifty-four seconds. Gatto hit the record with an extremely low dwell ratio. Despite the short time that his hands were free, he was able to remain consistent. Like all jugglers, Gatto synchronized his limbs to move at the same frequency. This synchronicity is what made the vision of nine gravity-defying balls suspended in the air so hypnotic. Jugglers like Gatto don't watch the balls, they feel them leaving their hands and coming back.

A founder can juggle with low dwell ratios by letting go of his goal-oriented personality before he enters his house. He no longer needs to control the physical space, define how it looks and question how it is run. He is non-controlling without being aloof. He should be aware that he cannot afford to act as a superhero at home over the long run. A superhero who is not a husband and father first will fall. He will be brought down from his pedestal, his achievements will be nullified, and only his role at home or lack of it will matter. A founder will get three or maybe four years to work without needing to be concerned about the emotional health of his family. These four years of emotionally detached mission chase is a free pass but with an expiry date. After this free run, he better wake up to make up for lost time or cracks will appear. The difference this should make in the day-to-day life of a founder is that he should not treat his home like a rest camp. His house doesn't need a superhero who will fly around zapping problems to oblivion all of Sunday morning. So, what should he be if not the same hero as he is in the office? His home needs someone who is energetic, involved and in listening mode. Solving the problem is not as important as listening. His attitude with his family should not be 'oh, you will never get it, I will sort it out in a jiffy'. It should be 'I am here, tell me about your struggles'. The role of a spouse is underrated in a startup's journey but it deserves far more importance. Some spouses use their salaries to ensure financial stability in the early years. This itself gives the startup a chance to be born. The spouse has to take on a less demanding job to be able to be the primary person to run the house and raise the children. As the leads in this very critical task, they would also demand autonomy and not just the responsibility.

At home, the founder has to drop the high expectations they justifiably have in the office from their team. They have to consciously remind themselves that their home is not a startup where they have to prove something to everyone.

All of us are one person or nearly one person across our workplace and our home. We bring the same person to both settings. If we are dissatisfied in one place, we will create discord, have arguments and get into a tug of war with our partners. A founder's personality is imprinted with the need to change and build and fix. Their unhinged nature can wreak havoc at home if they are not conscious about who they are. The traits that make them successful in the outside world become a handicap in creating stability at home. A person on a four-year pass bringing their high-burn personality back home can be labelled an asshole by the very people who will become the most important people in their lives as the years go by. There will be disbelief that this strife at home is actually happening. The founder will argue with themselves that they are doing nothing wrong. Their personality and its intensity is hidden from them. When the discord becomes a part of life, they will find ways to fit it into their routine. Between Series A and Series D when their seven-year-old's voice breaks and they no longer want to be hugged, reality will come and bite hard. But by then, it will be too late.

A founder who can take out thirty minutes to remind themselves of their true nature will have a chance to hold it together. Being a spouse and a parent at home will require them to check their 'founder' tag at the door and enter their home without the trappings of a leader. They will interact and engage with the humility of a family-oriented person. They will use their power of communication to explain their challenges and wins and follies to their spouse and children, who will then see them as another human, not a founder, business leader or a person with substantial net worth. They must realize that at home, their personal success means nothing. The glory they will get in the end will be only theirs to savour and that too marred by the distance they would have created between themselves and those around them. A daily reminder of all this can keep a founder grounded in more ways than one. Thirty minutes spent in identifying their true nature to be same as the universal self will help them remember that they are neither founder nor householder. Identifying with the universe can ease the challenge in switching personalities from work to home to work. Not all mega founders figure out their homes as well as they figure out the inflection points in their vision. Something has to give and usually it's the relationship with those who we are closest to. This aspect of life is the casualty in the business of creating billions in startup valuation. For those who can work on it as single-mindedly as they work for their startup outcome, it will ensure their evolution not just to becoming better founders but also to becoming better humans.

12

The Untouched Macchiato

'In all my deeds may I probe into my mind,
And as soon as mental and emotional afflictions arise
As they endanger myself and others
May I strongly confront them and avert them.'

—Geshe Langri Tangpa (1054–1123),
Eight Verses for Training the Mind

The steaming americano sat silently in the white mug amidst the noise of the coffee machine forcing steam through roasted beans, laptop keys writing code and cranky children overdosing on sugary milkshakes. I took a large sip from it and paused the moment, allowing the liquid to lace the inside of my mouth. The single-origin Chikmagalur arabica filled my palate with its nutty berry-ness. It was Sunday and I was at Thirdwave Coffee's HSR Layout location for a meeting. Next to my coffee, the order number plate still stood like a clue marker at a crime scene. The glass walls partitioned the noise inside and the chaos of the traffic outside. The world outside slowly checked off its mundane list of Sunday chores. The waft of steam was ebbing as my coffee's entropy got better at mimicking the room. I was waiting for 'Been There Done That' or BTDT, a founder I had backed many years ago. BTDT had taken his startup public and was now living the glorious life of a successful founder who had seen many battles and overcome most of them. His delayed arrival was not because his startup had a burning problem that needed urgent addressal. Far from it. It had been two years since he had stepped off from running the ship. He had taken his startup to a public listing, appointed a CEO in his place and gradually removed himself from the day-to-day. From what I had heard, he had just joined a venture firm as an adviser, taking his mornings slow and his evenings even slower.

I was keeping an eye on the door for my founder friend and watching the regular stream of customers looking for their relaxed coffee break on a Sunday.

BTDT had made one of the biggest venture-funded companies in India and was now giving back to the ecosystem as a seed investor and mentor. He had made mistakes, lost his bearings more than once, made more money than he or his future generations could spend and kept his sanity and family together through it all. BTDT was the Key in his team of co-founders. His energy was the main driver in the startup. It was rough in the first few years and one of his co-founders dropped out to go back to a corporate pay cheque. His startup was on its last three weeks of cash runway when BTDT borrowed capital against his house. He kept the lights on along with a team who believed in him. In his fundraise meetings, BTDT could speak of the future as if he had seen it and had talked of the IPO as if he had already rung the bell for the opening. Investors believed in his belief.

Until his sixth grade, his parents left him in their ancestral home to grow up under the care of his grandparents. The grandparents had all the time in the world to instil values with extra emphasis on honesty, cleanliness and self-control. His childhood was spent watching discourses on TV sitting next to his grandmother. He grew up solemn and religious. The government school in the village was a circus with raucous children held against their wishes in decrepit classrooms. His thoughtful nature was not a great fit with the environment and he was on the receiving end of countless masculinity-laced stressors. The Hindi teacher in the school became his daily tormentor, who took BTDT's excellence in all other subjects but Hindi as a personal insult. To him, BTDT was rich and spoilt with no purpose in life except to waste his father's money. To him, lifting boys by their earlobes was helpful in character building. Two years of personal insults and physical abuse shook BTDT's confidence in himself. His performance suffered and going to school became a torture. His grandmother stood like a rock-steady reminder of his capability. Her love showed up in waiting for him till he finished his lessons late at night, feeding him his favourite food and making him feel special. BTDT summoned enough strength to master Hindi by drowning out the screaming voice in his head that called him stupid and a dull student of his own mother tongue. His grandmother taught him the joys of poetry and he began to write some of his own. His performance came back up and he continued to outshine everyone at the village school until it was time to move back to his parents' house in Rohtak. The house was a perk allotted to junior engineers who had more abbreviations in their salary slips than zeros. It stood patiently in a row of whitewashed houses with red serial numbers stamped on their front wall. The housing campus of the state electricity board was a pleasant place to grow up in. It had a badminton court and a community centre.

Since he started understanding the world around him, he also gathered that his family ran into the bogs of withering monthly cashflow with alarming regularity. Scarcity triggered in him a need to provide. 'Don't die poor. Don't die poor.' He repeated this mantra to himself when he found himself frustrated with the limitation on desire that poverty imposed.

BTDT had been outstanding in every academically-oriented pursuit. He cracked board finals, Olympiads and the hardest entrance examinations. He was on the college basketball team and always proved himself to be the most valuable player. To push himself out from his comfort zone, he even joined the English debate team. He learnt to think on his feet. He won the national title and participated in the global finals in Boston.

No one knew that he had not spoken a full sentence in English until he had turned fifteen.

When he got done with college, a US company called Trilogy Software hired him from campus. Schlumberger made him an attractive offer too, but the job would take him far from India, so he refused. Trilogy was known for its high bar on quality of people. The peer group for BTDT was only getting better with every change. His boss at Trilogy had worked with the brightest and best from top US engineering schools. When I called his boss to get feedback on BTDT before my investment, he had this to say, 'He easily falls in the top 5 per cent of people I have worked with in my entire career across the US and India.'

I picked up my americano and mentally praised the barista as I worked my way through the velvety gold emulsion of crema to the black liquid below.

Just then the door opened and the noise from the street outside managed a quick peek inside before disappearing again. BTDT was here! He looked different. The paunch was gone, his hair was cut in a youthful style and his clothes fitted well. BTDT gave me a big smile as we spotted each other. As he made his way to the table where I sat, a couple of heads turned in his direction, the recognition steeping in. We shook hands and apologized for not catching up in more than two years. Adding the Covid years, it seemed like a lifetime. The conversation turned from current pursuits to the past. His eyes

lit up the moment I mentioned his early days of starting up.
Once a Key, always a Key, BTDT started sharing his 'Odyssey'
with the same enthusiasm as if it were still about to unfold.
I asked him why he put so much on the line when his startup
came close to shutting down. His gaze wandered to the ceiling
and he took his time to answer. 'The security of owning a home
never mattered to me. To my wife, yes it did, and convincing
her was the harder part. But I saw it as a very obvious exercise—
there is no comparison between risking losing a house to seeing
your startup survive to become the size of company you think
it would become.' Unseen turns brought the startup to a
precipitous drop. BTDT was about to close a fundraise from an
Indian venture fund that had been talking to him for months.
Without a warning, they bailed out, citing some head-scratcher
of a reason. Time had to be bought and time was very expensive
at that point. The world closed around BTDT in a death grip.
He went back to the office and gave a rousing talk at the town
hall, reminding his team about the importance of what they
were building. He felt better himself and called the banker
about taking a loan against his house. Funds from BTDT's
home mortgage gave them a lifeline of five months.

The startup survived the funding downcycle and raised
a small round that cost BTDT a lot of equity. He cut a big
piece of the pie to the new investor because their cheque
could turn the fortunes of the startup permanently. BTDT
knew the traction was real and the market growth was now

finally happening. BTDT owned 50 per cent more than his co-founders' combined shareholding. This seemed fair now that the onus of saving the company fell squarely on BTDT's shoulders. His co-founders had been instrumental in deciding and proving the rational plan. The customer had been defined and the product had been built for the use case that mattered to this customer. They delivered on engineering. A product that worked came to life. Their startup had gotten the adoption off from a cold start and numbers had kept growing in a way that proved that the need was real.

BTDT told me with a chuckle that they were a week away from burning out when the funds from the round finally appeared in the bank account. He remembered how thankful he was not to be forced to write off all that had been proven until that point and restart from scratch.

Normal behaviour after this scare would be to become conservative and push forward slowly and carefully. With funds in the bank for fifteen months of guaranteed existence and the rational plan proven, BTDT found it more appropriate to unleash his unhinged side. The near-death experience had given him the courage to think in wild, irrational leaps.

He wanted to take off like his childhood icon, Kalpana Chawla, who took a wild leap from Karnal to NASA. Karnal was only a two-hour bus ride from Rohtak, and his school took their science class to Kalpana's school in the eleventh grade. After listening to teachers who had taught Kalpana and seeing the classroom where she studied, the visiting students settled on the green lawns to eat their tiffins. They sat in awe facing the red brick school building. BTDT could feel the power of Kalpana's indomitable spirit. He felt the power of achievement and the will to achieve the impossible.

In establishing the irrational part of the goal, BTDT fell into a pattern of good delusion. He suspended the reality that held his startup to the ground. He detangled the limitations of where resources would come from and how big this could get. He reset his customer footprint to jump from India to global markets. His pitch now sounded a bit vague, but he had enough proof points to weave the dream.

The first audience of this reality distortion was the leadership team that he set about putting together. At that stage, no proven business leader was interested in a little, unknown startup with funding less than their annual advertising budgets. BTDT was not pitching this puniness—he was selling the $1-billion-revenue company that he conjured up at will from his words. The believability was high and the listener was left seeking a ride in the bus. BTDT brought in a heavyweight from Unileaver to run sales at a salary higher than he paid himself and some equity to close the deal. The Unileaver hire asked his friend for ideas on how much equity he should ask for. His friend googled the question. The friend then conveyed Google's answers with so much confidence that there was no doubt that BTDT owed him at least 7 per cent of the equity. Why? In

BTDT's view, it was important to get Unileaver but 7 per cent was also expensive, irrespective of the situation. The negotiation ran into an impasse, but BTDT turned it around by breaking it into two parts—an upfront number of 3 per cent that would be worth $10 million in three years and $20 million in five years. This would outsize any other compensation expectation that Unileaver could imagine from anywhere. For Unileaver, a $10 million upside could give him f-you money to retire and take as many Europe vacations as he wanted and a dream home in any metropolis he chose to settle in. Unileaver told his wife the night before he signed the offer letter, 'If nothing else, I have a chance to be part of history.'

We had been chatting for twenty-five minutes and BTDT had not touched his full-size iced caramel macchiato. It just sat there. A scrumptious cold dessert in a frosted glass. Its caramel strands lining up inside the glass, beckoning surreptitiously for a sip and then a gulp. But it stood untouched. I wondered why he had ordered it if he was not going to drink it. Is he going to let it go to waste? My attention, momentarily fixated on the coffee, found release when BTDT got up to wave to the next customer who walked in. It was Unileaver himself. BTDT had set up a catch-up with Unileaver, after our meeting.

Unileaver was now running the business as the CEO. He had stuck around for his $20 million and also got a co-founder tag after a few years. Turned out that one of the co-founders was done with the roller coaster and lost faith in the journey.

The near-death experience had taken different tolls on different people. He went off to work at Honeybell and now ran a global business out of Bangalore. The gap he had left was filled by Unileaver. I had seen Unileaver bring in the systems that married the plan to execution. Without him, BTDT would not have taken the flywheels as they appeared in the business. The net worth in the café was now in triple-digit million dollars!

Between the three of us, the topic shifted to the car that BTDT now drove. He had gone through a series of outrageously expensive German beauties that he realized were too impractical for Indian roads. He said he was now down to two cars between him and his wife and they were both electric SUVs. His wife was looking for furniture for the new house and he had hitched a ride with her to the coffee shop. Unileaver was happy with his silver Mercedes SUV. He took a different table and we continued our chat.

We went back to how the irrational part of his goal was achieved. BTDT was a master storyteller and used analogies like a poet. Maybe the hours of childhood TV spent watching gurus give discourses to a spellbound audience taught him some valuable lessons in rhetoric. BTDT could hold a room rapt in attention when he spoke. His audience followed his narrative visually, creating pictures in their mind as he described the new world. His dream had reached the ears of an oracle in a far-off land who was always looking to back young people brave enough to create a big change in the world and also good at articulating it. He had sent his scouts to recce the land for mega founders and screen the most humongous of goals.

The scouts told BTDT that the oracle would like to meet him and his co-founder at his headquarters. BTDT packed his dreams and plans in a carry-on and jumped on a flight. The next night, he was appreciating the raw flavour of yellowfin tuna deftly sliced by the oracle's private chef. The chef could have run a Michelin-star restaurant anywhere in the world and here he was, laying out a variety of finely crafted dishes in handmade ceramic dishes to a boy from Rohtak. The night was long and the audience of one was attentive. This pitch was not the standard one. The one that raises $10 million or $20 million. This pitch was to fund the big dent in the world. A $100-million cheque and many hundreds to follow. BTDT had taken an overnight flight after weeks of pushing intense growth and new product launch work. He should have been on a vacation but instead, he was making the pitch of his lifetime. The day had been packed meeting executives from the investment company. BTDT had already been speaking for the last eight hours by the time he reached the massive villa on top of the hill. His energy was still at a peak. There was not a trace of exhaustion in his body or his speech. The pitch of his life was as awe-inspiring as his town hall address or his dream weave for Unileaver. The oracle could see a founder who had the potential to change the world. The pitch worked and the flight back was the first time in a year that BTDT slept like a man with no care in the world.

BTDT was single when he started the business. He got married when the startup turned three. His co-founders got married. One became a father in those four years and thought about household budgets for the first time. At the time he flew to meet the oracle, his startup was surrounded by three nearly similar replicas funded by other investors, some nipping at their ankles, some winning customers faster than them. The BTDT I first met was a young passionate man with zeal and excitement. By the time he exited the business, his family had grown to four, he had become 'middle-aged' and he had lost his grandmother and his father. Both passings had left a deep hole in his heart.

BTDT did a good job pacing himself on the long journey and addressed his gaps in time before they caused irreparable damage to the startup. The personal journey took him face to face with his demons. His trust issues caused a lot of pain to people around him. His relations with his co-founders had taken a toll with constant fault-finding and distrust in their commitment level. He had a public showdown with one co-founder after a fall and that set alarm bells ringing. One board member suggested letting a coach identify the core of the issue and that was a breakthrough.

BTDT's attitude was amazing in his desire to fix. Not only did he implement the advice but he also put his heart into it. The coach went deep inside his head and found the emotional scar that the Hindi teacher had left. Identifying it was half the battle won. BTDT consciously worked on this awareness and reminded himself to be unbiased about trusting people around him. He started catching himself being unfairly accusative. He appointed referees from his team who were assigned to point out his behaviour if he fell back to his pattern. It was an ego balancing exercise that did wonders for BTDT's approach to people.

BTDT and his co-founder got back to being a unified force. BTDT's leadership style also got a shot and he was comfortable delegating control to leaders like Unileaver. BTDT made use of this bandwidth release by visiting his customers across India. He had forgotten what customer love was. Now he was even more motivated to build a thriving business. He took time off from the day-to-day running to visit and meet people who could tell him how his startup could sell in new markets. He came back thinking of the next flywheel that would get the business to the next trajectory of growth.

The macchiato sat ignored. A fly soon found its way to our table despite the air curtain placed at the entrance whooshing angrily at every incoming customer. I got distracted again from the conversation thinking, what if the fly entered the macchiato? I started shooing it away with my hand and hit the straw instead. The tall macchiato tilted over and finally rested on its side. The light brown liquid slowly spread on the table between us and some found itself on my white shirt.

I started lamenting my clumsiness and my bad luck with white shirts. I apologized for the mess I had caused. My bourgeois mind pointed out that the mess of overpriced sugar, coffee and milk was worth Rs 500. BTDT looked unperturbed. He walked over to the counter, asked for help cleaning the mess and paid for a replacement of another tall caramel macchiato. He came back and we just moved to another table. The early version of BTDT would have been as hyper about this as I was. Over his years of dealing with much bigger falls than this spill, he had achieved equanimity around all kinds of situations. In the early years, whenever there was a fall, BTDT would turn into a monster who would go around biting people's heads off. The development team was at the receiving end every time the app went into a 'not responding' mode for millions of Android users. BTDT's cortisol levels were high for long periods, causing his physique to change from a lean sportsperson to someone with baggy eyes and a big paunch. Once these panic-causing falls became more frequent, he subconsciously started responding with 'ugly coping'. This response mechanism helped him in dealing with the fall by negating it but as a side effect, it inflated his ego. As he matured as a founder, BTDT began to rely on the spiritual aspect of the world (thank you, grandma). He learnt to have what can be called now 'the beginner's mind'. He could step back from a fall and see it as a very forgivable outcome because he replaced the concept of success and failure with the notion of forward movement. Now he was able to do more. He rarely felt shy of trying brave new solutions and didn't even need to bounce back because he didn't feel like there was a fall.

As an investor, I felt that BTDT was one of the most live-wire founders I have ever backed. In his twelve-hour day he touched all employees, kept his investors well informed and picked up customer insights. He knew precisely what questions to ask that would help move things forward on multiple fronts. The hardest problems kept boiling up to him but he learnt to process and pass it back. He optimized his time by thinking through the solution and handing it off to an owner as quickly as he could manage. He remained on top of things and in the seven years that I was on his board, he remained unfazed with the number of things on his plate with lots of room to take on more. Through his workday, BTDT renewed his energy with timeouts to play quick rounds of basketball. Once a week, he had a planned drinking session with his team. The quantity of alcohol consumed in it reduced as the startup aged but the age of the alcohol consumed increased progressively.

I used to visit the startup for board meetings and was greeted by the crazy excitement on the floor, with every team member buzzing in harmony. The office was on two floors—both open-seating areas. One which housed the product and engineering teams and another where the business and customer support teams sat. Both floors had a large screen that showed the key metrics scaling—the team would ring a bell if a milestone was crossed and BTDT would come to the floor to celebrate with them. A little jig would happen and everyone would go back to chasing those metrics.

BTDT's startup employees ended up owning an above-average stake in the company. Fifty-seven new millionaires got added to the wealth manager's target list when the shares were listed on the exchange. This, the regular destressing and the co-founder realignment made sure that BTDT could continue to produce and supply energy to the startup to grow from within.

I glanced over at Unileaver while BTDT finally took the first sip from the freshly replaced glass of macchiato. I breathed in relief. After some intense phone scrolling, Unileaver was beginning to look in our direction to check if we were getting done. BTDT and I still had ten minutes to go. Patience was not a quality you picked up working with BTDT. Some board members were perturbed by it. A few blamed him for bringing the company close to death by running too fast. I, on the other hand, admired that the most about BTDT—he set a fast pace in his execution and also valued it in his team. He and his co-founders had used every available playbook to race through the product design and development in the ninety days that followed their first funding round. The speed out of the door kept him ahead of the me-too pack that raised their seed rounds just around then. He got into pole position, closed the round fast and went out pre-emptively to put together the most kick-ass team in the market. The team was lean and the headcount remained below fifteen. Each member of this team was identified and personally sold the vision by BTDT. Competing startups had teams of fifty people and gloated about their 'growth'. They moved slower and went around in circles. His startup got the answer to the elusive product-market fit equation and got as good a handle possible on how much cash burn would result in how much growth. When the oracle found BTDT, he was told that BTDT was the best founder in the space.

We were getting ready to say our goodbyes. Naturally, the conversation moved to family and health. BTDT was still happily married with a successful startup built. During the early, days he was trying to remain grounded but all the hero worship he received in the echo chamber was not making it easy. The winner's effect had caused him to take a few expensive wrong calls. BTDT went back to the day one mindset and made it into a habit. He remembered the day he saw the pieces falling into place in his mind Tetris—he envisioned the product and made it into his destiny. The first few weeks of whiteboarding came with the vision of the final scale he wanted to achieve. Every time he caught himself gloating, he reminded how far he was from that goal. With some forced and unforced ego balancing, he was able to let go his work persona when he was at home. He let his wife lead the family-raising process while he became an eager follower. One of his sons was diagnosed with a learning disability at six. His wife had already taken a less demanding role at work but this additional pressure was taking a toll. Luckily, Unileaver's hire was proving to be a double blessing. It gave BTDT enough extra bandwidth to take over some of the home duties.

We were now standing up, ready to shake hands and end the meeting. I asked BTDT one last question. 'Do you feel satisfied with all your accomplishments?'

BTDT's voice came from deep within without a pause. 'Not so much from accomplishment. We never had enough at home while growing up and I could have set myself up comfortably from a pay cheque. But I had to find something bigger to consume me. I never made a financial goal for myself because I knew nothing would satisfy me. I am glad I didn't. I loved the extreme highs and lows during the early years. For some time after I exited, I was trying anything that would give me the same buzz. I started running, trained for marathons and then ultramarathons. I challenged myself to run seven marathons on seven consecutive days on seven continents. I managed five. I was dehydrated and sick but I kept running. Everything I did after the startup was enjoyable for a while but the joy did not last. No achievement was big enough. Until I just gave up on linking satisfaction to achievement. I got operated for a running injury and had time to think. I believe that I had this force inside me that needed to be spent. If I didn't do it, it would have destroyed me. I think the outcome was just a stroke of luck. It could have gone anywhere. It was the wild, wild journey that consumed the force. After the crazy ride, I don't think I need to do anything more to spend it. I feel peaceful inside. And I feel happy that so much wealth got created in the process.'

After that long answer, he picked up the macchiato, downed it in one gulp and let out a satisfied sigh.

Acknowledgements

I am not a founder. I have started two venture firms from scratch, if that counts. I did have days when I tried to steer my mind away from doomsday thoughts about failing to raise the first fund. Disappointment smiled from dark corners, mocking my efforts and the futility of action. Swinging between hope and despair, I briefly experienced the volatile world of the real tightrope walkers—founders, of whom I have seen thousands and worked closely with hundreds as their financial backer, champion and self-appointed therapist. I have had the luckiest seat in the world—the front row of startup action with founders duking it out with fortune, luck, chance or whatever form it came in. I have seen the person who set foot on the tightrope and I have seen the person who stepped off. Two different people. The rope changes you and makes you approach life differently. In these high-stake walks, I have seen behaviour patterns that I could link to important outcomes, such as shareholder value, longevity of business and early burnout. I observed things that the founders said or did or wished they had done or not done. The list sat in my head as I watched batch after batch of new founders take the tightrope to the moon.

When the idea of this book popped up in discussions with my editor, it looked like nothing but an elaborate scheme to embarrass myself. It is a fool's mission to link business outcome to human behaviour. Not only are we talking about everyone's favourite topic but one where any theory can be disproven with endless exceptions to the rule. Despite the hesitation, the subject of identifying any sort of pattern in founder traits got my mental juices flowing. Like a good venture capitalist, I decided to take my chances. In this book, I have put my thoughts on the mindset of winning founders. I am ready for a good takedown that would critique these traits as blasé, old wine in new bottles or too generic to apply.

While I tried to remain politically correct with a gender neutrality, I must admit that I mostly drew upon my experience with male founder behaviour. I can safely say that any women founders reading this book would find it amusing at best. My data set has been mostly limited to male founders and I hope I can write a new book on female founder traits in a few years. Nevertheless, I hope women founders who do read the book can forgive this ignorance and can still take away something worthwhile.

I have worked with so many incredible founders who have had their battle days, their victories and routs in public view, teaching me along the way how they felt and how they coped. I am grateful for their honesty and grace. In discussing the thoughts behind each trait, I have brainstormed for many hours with friends who are founders or investors. Those who gave their precious time include Subrata Mitra, Dinesh Agarwal, Arnav Kumar, Amod Malviya, Naveen Tewari, Ramakant Sharma, Pratik Agarwal, Zishaan Hayath, Vivek Gupta, Nishchay AG and many others.

I would like to thank my family. My children, Nandini and Varun, who finally read my previous book, *The Moonshot Game,* and gave critical feedback. You two are my best investments. My wife, Vandana, who has always believed in me and encouraged me to take uncharted journeys like Arkam Ventures. You are my anchor and biggest strength.

I hope this book is helpful in revealing the mindset that founders carry with them as they shape the world. I wish every founder more power and balance as they make their journeys on the tightrope to the moon.

Scan QR code to access the
Penguin Random House India website